OVER THE HILL
to the
SUPER BOWL

Brig
OWENS

Chuck
CASCIO

OVER THE HILL
to the
SUPER BOWL

Robert B. Luce, Inc.   Washington—New York

Copyright © 1973 by Brig Owens and Chuck Cascio

All rights reserved, including the right to reproduce this book or parts thereof, in any form except for the inclusion of brief quotations in a review.

Library of Congress Catalog Card Number 73-9053
ISBN 0-88331-061-9

To my wife Patti and my two girls and my parents, for without them life would be meaningless.
Brig Owens

To Bonnie, Ross, Marc, family and friends—thanks.
Chuck Cascio

The photographs on pages 128 (bottom), 145, 186, 187, and 188 (top) were taken by Chuck Cascio.

ALL other photographs are Paul Fine Photos, courtesy of Nate Fine Productions.

Preface

It started in 1971 when George Allen became head coach of the Redskins and immediately began trading draft choices for veterans. Names like Pardee, Pottios, Petitbon, Biggs, Jefferson, McDole, and Kilmer had been heard around the NFL forever, or so it seemed. Some of the players had been All-Pro at one time or another; some had been on championship teams in the past; some were just known as tough competitors. However, to hear people talk, you would have thought that these players needed blood transfusions to get up in the morning.

The "Over the Hill Gang" became the term used to describe the Redskins. We were looked upon as a collection of has-beens who would undoubtedly try hard, but fail in the end. When we lost in the first round of the playoffs in 1971, the response seemed to be, "Well, those old fellas just ran out of steam. It had to be expected." We were given up for dead.

The corpse arose last year. 1972 was a season of challenges. We overcame the World Champion Dallas Cowboys. I regained a job which appeared lost. And the whole time the critics were reminding us that we were all a year older. But we also had a year's worth of playing experience together—we knew the coach, knew the system, and knew one another better than the previous year. And we put everything together.

We went to the Super Bowl, and only one other team did that.

True, we lost to that other team. But it's safe to say that the "Over the Hill Gang" returned from the dead. It just didn't collect its final reward.

Contents

The Beginning	1

Pre-Season

The Baltimore Colts	15
The Denver Broncos	19
The Philadelphia Eagles (1)	23
The Detroit Lions	26
The Miami Dolphins	28
The Pittsburgh Steelers	31

The Season

The Minnesota Vikings	35
The St. Louis Cardinals (1)	43
The New England Patriots	53
The Philadelphia Eagles (2)	59
The St. Louis Cardinals (2)	67
The Dallas Cowboys (1)	75
The New York Giants (1)	85
The New York Jets	95
The New York Giants (2)	103
The Atlanta Falcons	113

The Green Bay Packers (1) 121
The Philadelphia Eagles (3) 129
The Dallas Cowboys (2) 137
The Buffalo Bills 147

Post-Season

The Green Bay Packers (2) 157
The Dallas Cowboys (3) 173
The Super Bowl 189

The Beginning

Summertime at Dickinson University campus in Carlisle, Pa., is synonymous with work and heat to Redskin players. I arrived there for the seventh time in mid-July, 1972 and it hadn't changed. Sweat poured off my body as I walked leisurely. I knew all the time head coach George Allen would be saying, "Ahhh! This is Redskin weather." Of course, for Coach Allen *any* weather is Redskin weather.

I came early enough this year to watch our rookies scrimmage with the Philadelphia Eagles rookies. I moved in and made sure the indispensable air conditioner was working, then roamed around the dorm to see if any other veterans had arrived. Chris Hanburger, Charley Taylor, and Tommy Mason were all checked in. We were all anxious to see the rookies play, so we got a quick hamburger and went over to the field.

On our way to the scrimmage, we shared our fears about having to get into shape. There's nothing worse. If a man wants to make a million dollars guaranteed, let him discover a pill that could get football players into playing condition. Guys would pay anything for it.

I make it a point to be in fair shape when camp opens; otherwise training camp is a very slow death. There's too much physical and mental strain on a player in camp for him to be saying to himself, "I wish I'd worked out earlier."

At the scrimmage, quite a few other veterans were waiting to watch the rookies play, a lot of them naturally curious to see who was in their spot and just what kind of competition they were up against. As the veterans laughed and joked, I sensed a certain air of confidence. We came early for more than just the rookie scrimmage; deep down we're anxious to get started for what we feel will be *our* season. Everyone wants to be a part of this year's team because there's the feeling that it's going all the way.

In 1971, George Allen's first year in Washington, the Redskins had their best season in 29 years. We won nine, lost four, and tied one, and then lost to San Francisco in the league playoffs. It was the first time since 1945 that a Redskin team had been in the playoffs.

Our record last season was achieved despite crucial injuries to first line players such as Sonny Jurgensen, Jerry Smith, and Charley Taylor. They saw action for only part of the season. Larry Brown was hobbled by injuries for much of the year although he missed only one game.

This year we feel we are even stronger. Sonny, Jerry, Charley, and Larry are all healthy again, and it seems we will have more depth at every position. In fact, last year's replacements for those injured players are certainly not going to give up without a fight. Billy Kilmer, for one, quarterbacked our team to last year's historic marks, and he's looking for that number one spot again this year.

Manny Sistrunk was at camp early, too. We call him "Super Sis" because of his tremendous strength. He has arms like two tree trunks, and he's certanly one of the strongest men in the game. I was immediately impressed with the shape he was in. And I know that's good. With his strength and quickness and last year's playing experience, he can be one of the best defensive tackles in football.

Also looking in absolutely great shape was Jim Snowden, known as "Snowman." We've been teammates for seven years now and we both feel seven will be our lucky number.

I hardly recognized a long-haired, mustachioed dude standing next to Snowman. It was Leonard "Zeke" Hauss, our quick starting center. He was being playfully pushed around by our other "Zeke," tackle Walter Rock. Jerry Smith, my roommate for six years, arrived shortly after I did. It was the first time he's ever been early for camp, and I swore it would cloud up and rain instantly. Sure enough, just before the end of the scrimmage, a thunderstorm hit.

In all, about 80 percent of the veterans were early and we weren't pleased with what we saw in the rookie scrimmage. John Reaves, the Eagles' rookie quarterback from Florida State, did an excellent job of penetrating our rookies' defense. Everyone knows that the Redskin defense is George Allen's pride. Coach Allen is a very poor loser and he and the veterans are rather disgusted with the rookies' defeat. We don't want to get started on a losing note, even in a rookie scrimmage.

George Allen doesn't have too much patience with rookies. Once his veterans get into camp, he starts to assume things. He figures we know what we have to work on to improve ourselves, so he doesn't have to teach fundamentals to veterans. At my position, safety, I know through experience what offensive moves to look for that will indicate a certain play.

Although a rookie may have played a lot of defense in college, he's still not nearly prepared for what Coach Allen is going to throw at him. The Redskins have the most complicated, sophisticated defenses in football, and they demand too much for any rookie to know in advance. We have to know how to play the various defenses and *why* we're playing them.

Although I know it's tough on the rookies, I can't honestly say I feel any sympathy for them. They're out for my job, and I'm out to keep it. I can't afford to be telling a rookie my secrets about how to play the game. Occasionally, if a rookie looks like he might be a real asset to the team, I'll give him a little advice. Other than that, he's on his own.

My own experiences as a rookie weren't all that great. I came out of the University of Cincinnati as a quarterback who had been fourth in the nation in total offense and went to the Dallas Cowboys as a seventh round draft choice in 1965. The Cowboys said they'd give me a shot at quarterback, but somehow I felt the chance of being the first black quarterback in pro ball wouldn't come with a Texas team. I was right. After a few days of practice, Coach Landry told me to meet with the defensive backs. I'd never played a minute of defense in my life. So the first thing they had me do was get in the nutcracker drill. Who did I have to hit head-on but Don Perkins, many times an all-pro fullback. I hit him as hard as I could and he went down but I saw stars.

Ernie Kellerman, an old college rival of mine who'd quarterbacked for the University of Miami in Ohio, was a rookie with Dallas the same year in the same situation. He had to hit huge Amos Marsh. That night Ernie said, "Brig, are you sure you want to go through that every day?"

I shuffled my aching bones around a little on the bed and thought it over. Eventually, I said, "Ernie, let's stick around a little longer and see how it goes." Ernie wound up starting at safety for Cleveland, and I wound up in Washington after a year on the Dallas cab squad.

That rookie year is always tough. It always will be. No rookie has time to do anything other than study his play book in his spare time. He can't be lounging around or visiting other guys' rooms because he just won't be a pro for long.

By 6:00 p.m. dinner the night of that rookie scrimmage, the veterans were laughing and joking, saying how they dreaded tomorrow's practice which marked the beginning of our two-a-day workout sessions.

After dinner, we held a meeting where everyone introduced themselves. The gleam in Coach Allen's eyes showed that he was happy the veterans had arrived. He's an enthusiastic man and the condition of the veterans added to his fervor. He delivered a brief pep talk aimed at one thing — Super Bowl, 1973. That night we all watched a television special called "Three Cheers for the Redskins," which featured last year's season. It was a pleasant way to end the first day — the only pleasant day we would see for several weeks.

We all have one thing in common at the end of the first day of practice — we're all dead. It gets worse before it gets better. During the second day, on top of a two-and-a-half hour workout, we ran 24 wind sprints — 12 in the morning session and 12 in the afternoon.

After a few days I didn't feel too bad because I'd arrived in good shape. Last season I had an aggravating knee injury that slowed me down. I also had a lingering rib injury, so I got into shape in the off-season. Since Coach Allen traded for Rosey Taylor, his safety with the Bears, I knew I had to be ready to play competitively to defend my job when the camp opened this year.

Coach Allen knows how to get a team rolling. There's always a lot of running. The first week is devoted to agility drills, ball handling, and acquainting the defensive players with our defenses. Of course, this makes it that much tougher on rookies who haven't had a season to become familiar with the plays.

We have two weeks of two-a-days and one of one-a-days before we play Baltimore in our first exhibition. Toward the end of the first week, some of the veterans start the countdown, which will continue until the grueling two-a-days end.

At the end of a hard day's work, the team likes to have a little fun in the dining hall. Team camaraderie helps make winners. In order to get up that spirit, we like to hear the rookies sing. Jim Snowden shows them how it should be done. He gets up in a chair, gives his name, school (Notre Dame) and position (offensive tackle), then sings the famous Notre Dame fight song in a booming baritone. He puts so much into it that before long everyone in the dining room is singing. However, when their turns come, the rookies get the silent treatment. No one sings with them, and if they're not up to par they get booed pretty soundly. As might be expected, not many have good voices, although occasionally there's one who can stave off the boos.

There's a relationship between how a rookie accepts his singing responsibility and how he acts on the field. If he's enthusiastic about his singing, he's likely to play the game the same way. Coaches and veterans alike will judge a rookie initially on how he approaches his song, so it is quite important for a man trying to make the club to show some spirit. This year, not one rookie could sing. Even after Snowden's bravura performance, they flopped. I don't know what's happening to these young kids today.

Our work days at training camp don't end with the fun and games at dinner. After dinner we all have one or more meetings to attend. The meetings are broken down into general, specialty teams, defense, and offense. After offense and defense separate, the components of the two groups split further — defensive line, defensive backs, offensive line, offensive backs and receivers go to their own special meetings.

By 10:00 p.m. all meetings are over and we have some free time. Guys spend it studying, talking, watching television, writing letters, and trying to talk on the telephone. I say "trying" because only one phone is available and there's always a line waiting to use it. Consequently, the man on the phone is subject to a good deal of harassment from those who are waiting.

Then there are those players too tired to do anything but lie flat on their backs in bed. My roommate is a charter member of that crew. To be honest, I'm generally in bed early myself; not a bad idea when faced with a seven o'clock wake-up. Breakfast is from 7:30 to 8:00 a.m.; anyone missing the meal is fined five dollars.

One guy who's regularly awake before wake-up is Super Sis. He has a unique sense of humor. His idea of fun is to get up early and grab breakfast before anyone else. Then he returns and bangs on doors until he has company. Understandably, not too many players share in the laughter he gets from it.

During the second week of camp, we got our first bad injury. It happened to Snowden, a very important part of our offensive line. What's worse is that it was a freak accident: he was pass blocking and all of a sudden his knee gave way on him. He went down and just couldn't get up. Everyone had to feel sorry for him lying flat on his back when he was counting on a great, great year. Now it's doubtful that he'll play at all this season.

Injuries can plague a man mentally as well as physically. I refuse to let the thought of injuries weigh on my mind, for they occur when you start worrying about them. I try to play this game with abandon. There is never any reason to let up in any game. If you do, you can't go out and play your best.

That's how you get hurt and how you lose.

But Snowden's case was a freak. He hadn't given up; he hadn't lost his abandon. He just hit the ground and couldn't get up. Just like that and he's out indefinitely.

Sometimes people wonder if a player who really gets hit hard becomes shy. As far as I'm concerned, I'm determined after every good hit to ring my opponent's bell even harder next time.

Coach Allen immediately began looking frantically around the country for someone to replace Jim. Several names were tossed around including Dick Schafrath, a standout tackle with Cleveland for many years. Allen finally persuaded a former Redskin and close friend of mine, Mitch Johnson, to come out of retirement. It's ironic that Jim and Mitch were roommates while with the Skins.

George Allen knows Mitch Johnson's talents well. After Mitch dislocated his hip with Washington in 1968, he was traded to the Los Angeles Rams, who, of course, were coached at that time by none other than George Allen. Mitch should help our club because not only is he a fine tackle, he's a good guard as well.

About the middle of the second week, everyone's body is so torn down from two-a-days, they're just about crazy. Guys are praying for snow and some of the more delirious fellows are wondering about the possibility of a huge outdoor air conditioner. They figure if anyone can arrange it, Coach Allen can.

Although Ron McDole is a natural comedian the heat brings out the funniest in him. One day he was going around the locker room dancing on his toes like a ballerina. Being 6'4", 270 pounds, he's not exactly the most graceful figure. He's also been doing his imitation of a cat and dog fight. And he's come out with a few surprise elephant yells which caused more than a few players to jump off the locker room benches.

Another diversion from the grueling two-a-days has been the Washington Redskins Intrasquad Chess Tournament. This event was spurred on by the Fisher-Spassky World Championship, and competition has been fierce. John Wilbur, better known as "Strange," set up the tournament. The stakes are high — the winner will receive a color television set. Everyone is trying to play chess, even if he's never played before. And everyone swears he's a champion at it. Wilbur himself has bought three books on it, and he hasn't won a game yet.

Speedy Duncan arrived in camp two weeks late and everyone is teasing him. We all want to know if he got enough money. Speedy talks right back. "I own this ball club now," he says. "And, by the way, watch your mouth." Although we rib him, the players feel it was between Speedy and the management. Any man is entitled to what he can get, and players respect that right.

It's County Fair time in Carlisle at last. The Fair comes once a year just about the same time our two-a-days are over. Perfect timing. Guys are feeling better, and getting more rest and the Fair is a tremendous outlet for training camp tension.

That Fair must see us coming every year. They have everything imaginable. By sheer coincidence I'm sure, they have a football game played with dice where you roll for a touchdown. Usually on the first roll, the fella running the game lets you get 95 or 96 yards and you try to score a touchdown. If you score, you win a hundred dollars, but I don't remember anyone winning over the years. Guys will drop money night after night with no luck, investing a hundred dollars or more trying to win.

The Fair has go-go joints, strip joints... you name it, they've got it.

Larry Brown has two huge stuffed dogs about four feet high in his room. He's conned everyone into thinking he won them, but actually he gave a cashier an autographed sweatshirt for them.

Snowman has returned to camp with a cast on his leg. It's definite he'll be out for the year now. Although he can hardly get around on his crutches, he managed to make it to the Fair. Not only that, he came back with a stuffed dog just like Larry's. "I just had an argument with my girl," he explains, "so I won this to use as my make-up dog." Evidently he found out the cashier was on the take too.

As for me, I won (legitimately) three small dogs, one each for my wife Patti and my daughters Robin and Tracy.

Montgomery Ward trucks are not a usual part of the scenery during summer camp, so we were all curious when one drove up. The truck turned out to be loaded with ten-speed bicycles; a surprise gift to last year's players from Coach Allen. As for Coach Allen, he received a tricycle. Everyone immediately began racing around Dickinson's Tartan-Turf track. It was one comic scene with guys breaking chains and tires blowing out. Imagine, if you can, Verlon Biggs at 6'5", 280 pounds perched on top the small seat of a bicycle.

We were supposed to ride the bikes to and from practice. At first, guys guarded the bikes with their lives, but after a while they got a little careless. One night someone came through with a truck and stole about 15 bikes. About two days after the theft, someone called the dormitory and said anyone wanting his bike back could get it by calling a certain number. Now that took one helluva lot of nerve.

No one knew who stole the bikes, but we all teasingly accused the Redskins security agent, "Double-O" Boynton. In truth, if Double-O found a penny, he'd search for the owner. Everyone enjoys kidding him from time to time, and he takes it in stride. He maneuvers his own ten-speed and performs tricks in front of the envious players.

I thought it would never come, but we're finally preparing for the first exhibition game on August 4 against the Baltimore Colts in Tampa, Florida. All through those double days, there's nothing to look forward to but another day's practice. But now at last there's Baltimore.

The Colts have to be considered a great team. They have good personnel everywhere. Their defense is terrific and their offense is headed by John Unitas — need I say more?

Our spirit rides high with this first game in sight. We've got a good offense and defense ourselves, and our defense is concentrating hard on putting into practice our idea of dictating to their offense. If we can do that, we can control the game. We're anxious to test ourselves against a team like the Colts.

Just before we left to catch our plane for the Colts game, Diron Talbert paid early-riser Manny Sistrunk back. Diron stuck a pencil in Manny's door and slammed it shut. No one answered Manny's calls to help get the door free. But after a couple of minutes the dormitory walls began to rumble a little bit, so we opened the door. If we hadn't gotten Manny out of that room, he'd have shaken down the whole building. We don't call him Super Sis for nothing!

Washington fans come in all shapes and sizes.

George Allen at his intense best.

Pre-Season

The Baltimore Colts

August 4 — Tampa, Fla.

Everyone's on edge for this one. We know we're going to face a tough team with a winning tradition, while trying to get our own winning tradition established at the Colts' expense. We feel we've got the personnel to beat them, but it's going to be a long hard fight all the way. Everyone's well prepared on the Redskins. We like the idea of being up against a good football team right away, because it will give us a chance to test ourselves and get an idea of how good we are.

One thing in our favor right away is that Johnny Unitas is not going to start at quarterback. Carl Douglas, a black rookie quarterback, is going to be tested. The Colts hope for a lot from him. He's big with a good arm. Like most rookie quarterbacks, his biggest problem is that his passes are easily read.

Likewise, the Colts are getting something in their favor — Larry Brown isn't going to play for us. Coach Allen wants to keep Larry out of all but the last two exhibition games. Larry's a great back, and he doesn't need six exhibitions to be ready for the season. George Nock, the strong stocky halfback we got from the New York Jets, is going to take Larry's place.

He'll have Charley Harraway, our regular fullback and a fantastic blocker, in the backfield with him.

I was pleased to find out that I was starting at free safety. Until this point I didn't really know where I stood. Coach Allen has been playing Rosey Taylor at free safety and Richie Petitbon at strong safety on the first team. When he brought in a ballplayer of Rosey's caliber I was asking myself, "Did I do a good enough job last year?"

Mentally, I've been trying to keep myself up at all times. I keep thinking of the saying that "sorrow fairly colors life." Well, it's my life, and I'm determined to choose the color. I don't intend to lie down. Given fair competition, I feel the best man will get the job. Naturally, I'm high for the Colts' game.

The Colts didn't give us the game we expected. We came out strong and George Nock and Charley Harraway really ran on them. George had around a hundred yards rushing breaking loose for a couple of good-sized gains. The Colts' quarterback had a very tough evening. Our defensive line put great pressure on Douglas and he wasn't very effective.

I managed to pick on Douglas myself by intercepting one pass and coming close on two others. I dropped one all by myself, and on the other I had help from Harold McLinton, who knocked one away from me when he buzzed from his linebacker spot just as I made my move for the ball. "Thanks a lot, Harold," I thought, "that kind of help I can do without."

Coach Allen was pleased after our decisive 33-3 win, knowing Baltimore is one of the truly good teams around. Everyone shared Coach Allen's elation after the game. We voted him a game ball and we sang him the family song for game ball recipients, "hooray for George, hooray at last, hooray for George, he's a horse's ass. . ."

After returning to Carlisle, Coach Allen threw us a surprise by announcing that we had the next two days off. As soon as he said it, the cars roared away from the Dickinson campus, most of them on their way to Washington, a short two hours away. Carlisle's not the place for excitement once the Fair's over. It has one theater, one pool hall and a couple of little bars. Nothing to make you want to stay around.

It had been nearly a month since I'd seen my wife Patti and my two little girls, Robin and Tracy, so I chugged home as fast as my blue Volkswagen could take me. My youngest daughter, Tracy, is just beginning to walk and talk so I'm anxious to see her progress. And Robin, who's four, always has many interesting things to tell me.

At home we didn't do anything out of the ordinary. I relaxed and licked my wounds and we went picnicking and swinging at a playground. I did wrestle a lot with Robin who is a very aggressive child. When she starts wrestling with her Daddy, Tracy wants to jump right in and eventually Patti does too, so that before long the whole Owens family is on the floor rolling around. That's how I spent much of my two days off. We all enjoyed it, especially me.

The trip back to Carlisle always seems longer than the trip to D.C. Your mind works on you because you know there's practice waiting at the end of the trip. Most dreaded are the 14 striders to run when we get back. Striders are 40 yard sprints we run with our units with about a 10 second rest in between — Coach Allen calls them "good ol' striders." An apt name — they tire you out quickly and make you feel very old.

As we begin preparing for our next exhibition game against Denver, a lot of veterans are talking about one rookie who's looking rather special. He's Herb Mul-key, a smallish (5'10", 175 pounds) running back who never even went to college. Coach Allen spotted him in the spring among several hundred hopefuls who attended an open try-out camp at RFK Stadium in Washington. Herb was recommended by Harold McLinton who saw him play with the semi-pro Atlanta Packers team. In fact, Harold lent Herb the money to travel to the D.C. tryout.

Herb impressed Coach Allen with a 4.4 second 40-yard dash and he hasn't quit running yet. He's been showing promise all training season and he's got a lot of determination. He's small, so some of the larger players have popped him hard. McLinton will hit Herb some good shots and say, "You sure you want to play here, little fella?" Herb just pops up and takes off again. Off the field Harold would encourage Herb. "Keep runnin', fella," he'd say. "Keep coming back for more."

When we have half speed drills, Herb goes full speed. When there's a call for players to act as our opponents, Herb's the first man there.

The biggest thing Herb Mul-key has going for him is that he's hungry for the game. I've seen a lot of players with more talent than Herb left out of football because they weren't hungry to play. Once a player loses that craving for football, he might as well quit. It carries players through the physical strain, and it's going to keep Herb Mul-key on the Redskins.

The Denver Broncos

August 11.

Days begin to go faster after that first exhibition game. Each week there's a game to prepare for and that makes the time move a little. This week it's the Denver Broncos led by Floyd Little, the former All-American running back from Syracuse University. Given the opportunity he can hurt an opposing team badly. But our philosophy is to dictate to their offense so they must play *our* game. We feel if everyone does his job properly, we should win handily. It's our first time this year before our great home crowd in Washington.

I'm eating my heart out with this game because I'm not scheduled to start. It's odd how this non-starter role is happening. Nothing has been said, but I can feel I'm losing my grip. I think I've done a good enough job during camp to get the chance to start, but for this game Rosey Taylor is starting at free safety with Richie Petitbon at strong safety. These two were the same pair of safeties who played for Coach Allen in the early sixties when he was defensive coach for the Bears. I know both positions extremely well, and while I'm disappointed, I'm not going to let it get me down. I've got to stay prepared so when I do get into a game I won't look like a fool.

That would be the worst possible thing I could do.

During the game, which we won 40-0, Richie hurt his knee and I took his place at strong safety. Right away we got the jump on Denver and they never got back into the game. It was one of those nights where everything clicks. With the score 33-0 late in the game, our third string quarterback, Sam Wyche, who is good enough to be first or second team on any club, took over from Sonny. Sam couldn't resist his inward urgings, and on his first play from scrimmage he fired a 52-yard scoring pass to Bill Malinchak, a wide receiver noted for his specialty teams play. After the game Sam told reporters he didn't want to be forgotten behind Sonny and Billy.

Our fans went wild and many of them were chanting "Super Bowl." Quite a few of the players were talking about it too, but I know we've got a long way to go.

Roy Jefferson got the game ball and our "horse's ass" chant. We have started to get the winning habit established in these early games. Coach Allen is happy about it because, as any good competitor knows, losing can become a habit too, and then a team's in real trouble.

On past Redskin teams we had guys who didn't care if we won or not. They had no idea of what was at the end when you win. They had no incentive and it really upset me to play with such guys. During a game things would start happening and they'd say, "Here we go again," and we'd drop another one. Any team can psych itself into a losing habit when things start to go bad. Some guys from losing high schools and colleges have no idea of consistent winning. Our coach at that time, Otto Graham, was a winner and fierce competitor, but he couldn't spread that competitive desire to the rest of the team. In time he might have, but it was Vince Lombardi who first gave the Redskins a taste of victory. He used to tell us, "Winning is one hundred percent elation and losing is one hundred percent resolution. The many physical hurts are a small price to pay for winning." There's too much work involved in football to lose a game. There's nothing in losing.

Coach Allen puts that same importance on winning. I never played on a losing team until I turned pro, so I'm anxious to help keep this year's winning habit going.

Coach Allen announced another two day vacation for us after the Denver game. Since we're already in Washington, we can all just go home. It gives me more time to spend with my little family, something I always look forward to. They're quite a bunch.

My tenacity is getting a good workout this summer and so is my roommate Jerry's. After being starters for six years, we're both being strongly challenged for our positions. My main challengers are Rosey Taylor, Richie Petitbon, and a rookie named Willie Germany. Jerry's getting pressure from Mack Alston who played tight end last year after Jerry was injured in our sixth game. Mack is about 25 pounds heavier than Jerry, and Coach Allen's giving him a good look. However, so far Jerry's still starting.

We've spent some free time discussing our situations over a couple of beers at a little pub called "The Bottom." One day this week he said to me, "Brig, I think I'm going to walk out of camp. I know I can play somewhere. I mean, I've been doing the job for six years and now I supposedly can't do it. I don't need this harassment, I know I'm a good tight end."

Listening to him made me stop and think. I know I can start with another team, but I said, "I know how you feel, but you just can't walk out of a situation. Look, you haven't been moved out of your spot. You're still in there and you can still impress them. I'm being treated like a rookie. I'm out of my spot, but I'm trying like hell to get back in. I'll tell you one thing — I'm not walking away from it."

It was Jerry's turn to think it over. Finally he said, "Yeah, you're right. You know, you always think you've got it bad until you see someone else's problems."

I knew Jerry wouldn't quit. But it's going to be a trying exhibition season for both of us. This team is loaded with talent. No one is unchallenged. Everyone's competing with proven veterans or good rookie prospects. At quarterback there's Billy, Sonny, and Sam Wyche, who is only 27 and a former starter for Paul Brown's Cincinnati Bengals. Our kick returners are Speedy Duncan and Ted Vactor, who handled the job last year, and Alvin Haymond, an all-time great who Coach Allen traded for while Speedy was holding out. Our two regular running backs, Larry Brown and Charley Harraway, have veterans Tommy Mason, Mike Hull, George Nock, and Bob Brunet behind them fighting for spots on the club. At linebacker, our starting trio from last year, Chris Hanburger, Myron Pottios, and Jack Pardee, are being pressured by veterans Harold McLinton, Rusty Tillman, and Rocky Rozema. Coach Allen puts the pressure on *everyone*.

We're preparing for the Eagles, our third exhibition opponent, Coach Allen making it clear that Billy Kilmer is his starting quarterback until Sonny beats him out. They performed equally well against the Colts and Broncos with Billy starting and Sonny playing the second half. Their statistics are almost identical. It does seem a shame that Sonny, one of the greatest quarterbacks ever, had to be hurt last year and miss out on a chance to play. Of course, Billy did an outstanding job to beat Sonny out for good. It's really hard to move a guy out once he steps in and does such a great job and wins for the team.

Dallas Coach Tom Landry once reportedly said, "There's no one in football who can throw like Sonny Jurgensen," and I agree. In all the years I've played with him, I've never seen him off. Sure, he misses receivers, but never by much. People say Sonny's never been a winner. The fact is, he's never played with a complete ball club — especially with a good defense that will turn the ball over frequently and give him good field position to work from, like we will this time around.

Billy Kilmer has faced much the same situation in his pro career with the Forty-Niners and the Saints. Last year he had his first opportunity with a complete ball club and he stepped in to do a great job. Billy made the most of it, he brought us to the playoffs and now Sonny's going to have to play himself back on to the first team.

Of course, the exhibition season is still young. A lot of things are going to happen, but for now it's Billy in the first half and Sonny in the second.

The Philadelphia Eagles (1)

August 18.

Everyone's up for the Eagles. They gave us fits last year; we beat them once and tied them once. They're a hard-hitting team that like to beat up their opponents. Last year they put Larry Brown out of our first meeting, which is a tough thing for any team to do. It's a grudge match whenever we play the

Eagles anyway. We feel we have to beat them convincingly because we play them twice in the regular season. It's a tremendous psychological advantage to beat a team badly the first of three meetings during a year. That second and third time are often a little easier, especially if we can dictate to them early.

Larry Brown wants to play in this one badly because he remembers last year. However, Coach Allen's going to have him sit on the bench again where he'll be until the fifth exhibition game or so. Larry can watch and think about what he's going to do to them during the regular season.

The Eagles have been trying to work in John Reaves, the rookie quarterback who beat our rookies in the scrimmage earlier this year. He's a fine passer, but in the professional ranks it's very hard for a rookie quarterback to step right in and do a good job. He has too much to learn about reading defenses. We plan to intimidate and confuse Reaves as much as possible.

It worked. We rolled up another big victory, 34-14, for three in a row. The game itself was rather sloppy, with a lot of penalties and mistakes. We intimidated Reaves as we planned and he got a close look at how this game is really played. Billy and Sonny again put in equally good performances. I didn't start, but I did see a lot of action and played well overall.

Excitement is mounting about our possibilities this year. But I keep reminding myself that it's still the exhibition season. With three preseason games to go, there's still that fear of injuries which can ruin a ballplayer and a team; most players and coaches dislike the long exhibition season for that reason. It wouldn't be so bad if the league would add the last two preseason games to the regular schedule, lengthening regular season play to 16 games. At least then the players could make a little more money and the risks would be worthwhile.

We accomplished our goal against the Eagles — beating them decisively in our first of three meetings. But they moved the ball on us at times and led 10-7 at one point. They're going to be tough in the regular season.

Three down, three to go and the Eagles were better against us than the score might indicate. We've got three tough teams ahead of us — Detroit, Miami, and Pittsburgh — and some tightening up to do.

For the second week in a row, it will be an intensely physical ballgame for us. The Lions will give our defense a crucial test. They have great personnel and we'll have our hands full. Their offense is explosive with Earl McCullough and Larry Walton at wide receivers and Charlie Sanders at tight end. Sanders will be my responsibility since I'm starting at strong safety. They have their choice of three strong running backs, Altie Taylor, Mel Farr, or Steve Owens. The Lions have an added dimension in that their quarterback, Greg Landry, can run as well as throw. Last year Landry set the single season rushing record for quarterbacks. On defense, Lem Barney at cornerback and middle linebacker Mike Lucci hold down a well-balanced unit.

The Lions will be ready to fire out at us because they know we've overwhelmed our first three opponents. They'll be determined not to be our fourth victim.

The Detroit Lions

August 25.

One common assumption about pro ballplayers is that the athlete on the road is on the make. An incident which occurred before playing the Lions in Detroit illustrates this assumption.

I was lying on my hotel room bed when I received a phone call from Mrs. Joanne Jones, an old school friend of Patti's and mine, who was in our hotel with Bill Triplett's wife. (Bill is one of Detroit's running backs.) I took both women out to dinner at Trader Vic's and we talked about old times and about our families. My teammates and quite a few other people eyeballed Joanne. Most people thought I had something going. Even if a ballplayer merely chats idly with a female, onlookers will assume he's hustling her. He can't just be friends with her. It's one of the problems of our society; we assume too much.

Just before the game I was told that I was starting, but only to play against Detroit's first offensive series. Then I'd be replaced by rookie Willie Germany who is a fine looking athlete. Coach Allen wanted to see what he could do in a game.

Willie confirmed Coach Allen's opinion that veterans

should be used whenever possible because they're less likely to make mistakes. Willie got beat a couple of times, resulting in long gains and a touchdown for Detroit. We wound up losing the game 24-10, but Willie was by no means the only reason we were defeated. In general, our defense broke down and the Lions moved the ball well against us.

Detroit capitalized on our mistakes and scored on some big plays. I had a good game, but what is a good individual game if you lose? It was our first defeat and, like any defeat, it was bitter. I'm a very poor loser. I try not to let anyone beat me at anything — cards, checkers, it doesn't matter — I hate to lose!

The game was beneficial in showing us we had quite a bit of work to do before we meet the Dolphins at RFK. We've got to get right back into that winning habit.

Mainly as a result of the Lions game, there is one less person competing for the safety position. Willie Germany failed in his make-it-or-break-it test. He was in a precarious position as a rookie facing Detroit's explosive offense. He's a good athlete, and I'm sure he'll catch on with some other club. Being on the Redskins this year as a rookie safety competing with veteran talent was certainly an unenviable situation. I think Willie knew after his Detroit performance that he was on his way out. For him, it was just a case of not being in the right place at the right time.

It's funny how things change. In my first couple of years as a pro, I'd keep my own roster of who was on the team and who was cut. All of the young and new players would scratch names off and we'd see the squad forming. When one of the other rookies was dropped we'd all get together and shake hands, mutter some encouragement and see him off. I'd have mixed emotions — sadness at seeing a friend go, but happiness at knowing that I was still around.

Now when someone's cut, especially someone new, I recognize it as just part of the game. I don't keep lists any more and I don't give any big good-byes, unless maybe it's a veteran I've played with for a few seasons. Veterans don't want any scenes made.

It's a cold game at times. When the Cardinals let Bob Reynolds go after a number of great years, all he got were his shoes. Some clubs aren't even that generous. If it ever happens to me, I'm just going to quietly disappear. I might say good-bye to my roomo, Jerry, but that's about it.

The Miami Dolphins

August 31.

Miami, Super Bowl contestant last year, is loaded with talent. Everyone knows about their Butch Cassidy and the Sundance Kid running attack. They've been using Mercury Morris a lot this pre-season, and he's capable of breaking away for long yardage. Bob Griese's a very versatile quarterback, and Paul Warfield is as fine a receiver as there is. Warfield undoubtedly runs his patterns more precisely than any receiver around. If a play calls for him to go down 10 yards, cut 41 degrees and back 21½ degrees, he'd do just that. The Dolphins could give us fits.

We're all determined. It's getting close to regular season play, and we want to get back on the victory trail. Our defense is ready and our offense is prepared to give a better showing than it did in Detroit. Larry Brown will play most of the game and that should give us a lift. As a team, we've got a lot to prove. We've been making too many mistakes and giving up some easy points and you can't win a championship that way.

We beat the Dolphins 24-21, but I must admit we were very fortunate to win. We made far too many mistakes. Our specialty teams broke down on punts and kickoffs; our defense went bad in spots and gave up big plays. We can't expect to play this way too often and come out on top.

I was fortunate to have another good game, grabbing two interceptions. To top it off, I received a game ball and it sure felt good. The team sang the usual horse's ass chant and I didn't mind being compared to that part of a horse's anatomy one bit.

Although we did play a sloppy game and I'm sure the Dolphins didn't feel they played well, it's good to make those mistakes and still come out on top against a team like Miami. I hope we're able to play them again in Los Angeles, the Super Bowl site, at the end of this year. Actually, I don't care who we play in Los Angeles, just so we're there. But I think Miami's got a great shot at it.

Since the Detroit game, we've been practicing at Redskins Park in Dulles, Virginia, a 20-minute ride from Washington, so we've been able to commute from home to practice.

Our half-million dollar facilities in Redskins Park are without a doubt the best in football. Coach Allen has everything conceivable there for us. There's a complete grass football field surrounded by a Tartan track. Next to it is a 100-yard astro-turf field. A huge tower is positioned between the two fields, so that our photographer Nate Fine can take films of practice. Inside there's a weight room, half-court basketball court, handball courts, and conference rooms lined with burgundy and gold carpet. Not just any kind of carpet, but carpet thicker than most people have in their homes. Coach Allen goes first class all the way. He's even installed a super-sensitive burglar alarm system to discover prowlers, spies and thieves.

At this point, with one exhibition game left, I feel I've had a good pre-season. In fact, it's the best I've ever had. I've reacted well to the pressure, and I hope it's good enough to retain my starting position at either free or strong safety.

My wife, Patti, knows my situation well, although we don't discuss it much. I don't bring my problems home, but Patti will sit down and watch films with me. I have family time and football time. She just keeps our normal routine, while I keep myself as prepared as possible in the fight with Rosey Taylor and Richie Petitbon for a starting job. One of us will be on the bench when the season opens.

In a move that created a lot of premature excitement, Coach Allen put Rosey Taylor and Myron Pottios on waivers this week. I'm not as happy as many people think I should be, because I'm sure they'll both remain on the team. Whenever someone congratulates me I just respond saying, "There's no big thing." I know I've still got a battle on my hands.

The Season

The Minnesota Vikings

Saturday, Sept. 16

By today, two days before our Monday night opener against the Vikings in Minnesota, we're ready. We've been waiting for this one because we know the Vikings are tough. But at the same time, there is an air of confidence that we are tougher.

Saturday practice was early, 9:30 a.m. to be exact, because Coach Allen went to see his son quarterback the University of Virginia against Virginia Tech. The practice was lively and the offense very sharp. Both Kilmer and Jurgensen threw well and our receivers have been catching everything thrown their way.

I'm convinced we have the best set of receivers in the business with Charley Taylor, Roy Jefferson, Jerry Smith, and Cliff McNeil. They've all been all-pro somewhere along the line. It helps the defensive backfield to practice against them, because when you get in a game any guy coming at you is not likely to be as good as they are.

Kilmer will start at quarterback against Minnesota. It's eating away at Sonny knowing he's going to ride the bench again. But Sonny hasn't let up; like all of us, he's waiting for his chance. Billy's been holding on, but Sonny's going to be hard to hold down.

Practice was over by 12:45 and I hustled to get dressed. I had a 1:30 date with Patti in Georgetown for lunch, shopping and people watching. People do such crazy things, they're great to watch. It's one of our favorite pastimes.

I date Patti from time to time, or send flowers unexpectedly—all of the little things I would do if we were still dating at Cincinnati. I think that's what keeps marriages going. You shouldn't take anyone for granted—especially your wife. As always my wife looked great. While we were out shopping we ran into Bill Malinchak. He was standing on a Georgetown corner by himself. Though I knew what he was up to, I asked, "What are you doin' out here?" He replied, "Girl watchin', cat, girl watchin'."

This evening my old roommate Lonnie Sanders dropped by and we talked football and business. Since his wife Anita was out of town, he stayed for dinner and Patti made two of the greatest T-bones around. That's living!

Lonnie left, and I spent most of the evening studying my scouting report on Minnesota. They're a good ballclub, no question about it.

Sunday, Sept 17

I'm a lucky man. Patti never lets me leave on a road trip without a good breakfast. So at 7:30 a.m. waffles, eggs, and sausages were waiting for me. As always before a trip, Robin and Tracy had breakfast with their Daddy.

I left the house at 8:10 a.m. although our plane didn't leave until 10:30. I had to pick up Tom Skinner, one of the most dynamic and true human beings I've ever been associated with. Tom rose from the street gangs of Harlem to become a minister. He spoke once at our team vesper services on Sunday morning and impressed Coach Allen and the players so much that now we have Tom at every service possible. He's become part of the Redskin family, and I'm glad of it.

We had a little time so we stopped at the Dulles Marriott for some coffee and bumped into Roy Jefferson and Mo Pottios having breakfast. They were both glad to see Tom, and we rapped about the team, politics and the Olympic games.

By 10:15, we were at Redskin Park boarding the bus for Dulles International Airport. Coach Allen has us ride the bus to and from the airport because last season we were frequently mobbed by enthusiastic fans. It was wonderful of the people, but we almost got killed. They hugged us and tore our clothes; I even lost a suit once when some girls tore the sleeves off my jacket. Traffic got so bad at times that the team stopped announcing arrival times because access roads to the airport got backed up.

Riding the bus, I thought of how important buses have been in our society. I thought about their significance in Montgomery, Alabama, and their impact in education today. We talk about how we must provide good schools for our children, but we sure don't want to pay the price.

Sunday is a long day when you play a Monday night game. After we got to the Twin Cities I sat around all day and watched other teams play on television. I paid particular attention to Green Bay vs. Cleveland because we play the Packers this year. They look good with two strong runners, John Brockington, last year's rookie of the year, and MacArthur Lane, whom they got from the Cardinals in a trade for Donny Anderson.

As I was heading into a 4:00 p.m. meeting, I noticed

Howard Cosell standing outside the meeting room. He was wandering around getting the feel of things and making a few comments. He's controversial, so he always draws attention. I think he's quite a person as well as a great sports commentator. Howard brings a lot of color to football, and that, in turn, has helped the players.

Howard's partner, Dandy Don Meredith, hadn't arrived yet. I would have liked to have seen him. He was the Dallas quarterback in 1965 when I was a rookie. We used to tease each other about which of us had the skinniest legs in football. Dallas never realized his value as a leader and quarterback until he was gone. They might have had a Super Bowl victory sooner if they had.

Players appreciate Don's coverage because he's so fair. He understands what goes on on the field. If a player misses an assignment, drops a pass, or throws a bad pass, Don may criticize, but he'll usually point out how difficult execution is in a game.

Coach Allen reminded us at our meeting about the need for our defense to contain Fran Tarkenton tomorrow. Coach Allen has had success against Tarkenton in the past and it's due mainly to his emphasis on the defensive backs sticking to their men no matter how much Tarkenton scrambles in his own backfield. We can't release our men too soon or else we'll be burned by a pass off the scramble. Coach Allen feels that although Tarkenton may get off a long run or two with his scrambles, the chances are they won't be as costly as a completed bomb. It's harder to make that yardage on the ground. We also intend to force Tarkenton to the sidelines when he scrambles. If we can trap him on the sidelines, we may force him to throw out of desperation and we'll come up with some interceptions. Tarkenton's not quite as quick as he used to be, and we feel we can pin him to those sidelines and contain him.

It's worked in the past; it should work again.

The meeting itself was relaxed — there was that air of confidence. Coach Allen was somewhat worried because he wasn't sure we were completely ready. But deep down, I think he knew we were.

Monday, Sept. 18

When you think of the Vikings, you have to think of their defensive unit anchored by Alan Page. Page is probably the best defensive lineman ever to play the game. Against us he had a pulled calf muscle and was in a cast the day before the game, but seeing him perform you'd never know it.

By game time Coach Allen had psyched us way up. I'm convinced the Redskins have pro football's best team togetherness. Our spirit is like a fever that spreads and everyone has it by the time we take the field. Grown men surprise you by acting as they do — shouting, clapping, talking nervously — everyone, even a non-starter like me.

We're a confident team because we know Coach Allen has made us the best prepared team around. Our preparedness paid off early in the first quarter when Bill Malinchak did his special thing — blocking punts. He picked up the ball and brought it in for a touchdown. Boom! Just like that we were up 7-0.

Late in the first quarter, Richie Petitbon, who started at strong safety, twisted his knee and I went into the game. Physically and mentally, I was ready, determined not to let my second-string status get me down. Standing on the sidelines, I watched carefully so if needed I'd be on top of the game. When I did get in, I played well — no mistakes and a few unassisted tackles.

The Vikings jumped ahead 14-10 after John Gilliam

caught a touchdown pass from Fran Tarkenton in the third quarter. But I was never really worried. I just kept going over our plays and personnel and I couldn't imagine them beating us.

Early in the fourth quarter, Billy Kilmer got the offense moving. A couple of passes to Jefferson, a few beautiful runs by Larry Brown and we were up 17-14.

On the kickoff following our seventeenth point, the specialty teams did it again. Bob Brunet clobbered the runner causing a fumble which Malinchak recovered. Charlie Harraway ran over for a touchdown making it 24-14.

Ted Vactor had blocked a field goal earlier, so the specialty teams were really something special tonight. It was a big lift because our specialty teams had been weak during preseason. But I think that was because so many rookies were on them then. Coach Allen has always preached that the specialty teams would win at least two or three games for us, and this was the first.

The Vikings managed to score once more, but it came with only a minute left to play. Actually, the officials gave them that one, because Oscar Reed never quite made it into the end zone. We complained, to no avail. People would be amazed at how much griping goes on during a game. Sam Huff was the biggest bitcher of all. If a play went by without Huff arguing, the officials would think something was wrong.

Anyway, we forced them to use a lot of time and the game ended 24-21. Although we gave up a lot of yardage for the night (over 350 yards total), the important thing is that we didn't give up anything long or quick. On that last drive, Tarkenton exchanged a few hot words with Mike Bass after Mike forced him out of bounds. Fran's a tough competitor, and when he's not winning it doesn't take much to irritate him.

After the game, the locker room noise was overwhelming

until Coach Allen quieted us down and we knelt and said the Lord's Prayer. I always give extra thanks for protecting both teams from serious injury and for letting us stick together as a team. We voted Malinchak and Coach Allen game balls and sang our usual chant. Chris Hanburger dubbed George the "Godfather of the Redskins."

On the noisy plane ride back to Dulles, that old feeling that victory brings was present. We were on top and everyone knew it. All the other teams would be gunning to knock us off, and that's just how we like it.

Specialty team captain Speedy Duncan was so proud of his team's contribution to the victory he was going around explaining where he got his personnel. "I started out in Uganda," he said pointing to various specialty teams members, "came through Egypt and went on to Sweden. I hopped over to Switzerland, picked up a couple of boys in Spain and finished up in Texas. Then I brought them all to Washington to play on my specialty teams."

We arrived at Dulles at 4:00 a.m. My eyes were burning, but I knew in less than an hour I'd be in the sack. Somehow, I knew I'd sleep well.

The so-called over-the-hill gang [Rosey Taylor (22), me (23), Chris Hanburger (55), Jimmie Jones (82), and Mike Bass (41)] in pursuit of Viking Clint Jones.

A happy Bill Malinchak, game ball winner and specialty teams hero of game #1, is congratulated by Speedy, me and others.

The St. Louis Cardinals (1)

Tuesday, Sept. 19

Have you ever felt someone staring at you? At 8:00 a.m., just three hours after arriving home, I opened one red eye and discovered I was right. From six inches away, Robin was staring at me.

"Hi," I muttered.

"Get up so we can talk," she demanded.

"Could you just give me a few minutes?" I croaked.

"Come on, Daddy, I missed you," she said unsympathetically." "Let's go drink some juice and talk."

I find it hard to say no to my little girls, so I'd started to get up when my wife came to the rescue. As Patti pulled her out of the room, Robin said to me, "O.K., Daddy, you get some rest for now and we'll talk later." She's something.

When I finally did get up, it was a typical off day. I didn't have any bumps or bruises, so I didn't have to go to Redskins Park at all. Any player who doesn't report a serious injury is subject to about a $100 fine.

That night, Ted Vactor, Mo Pottios and I spoke at a father and son banquet in Virginia. Ted gave them his Bill Cosby routine on specialty teams and he had them all rolling.

After the banquet we all went to the weekly Tuesday night team party. It's good for team togetherness and communication, something every team needs both on and off the field.

I didn't stay long at this party. I still wanted that bed.

Wednesday, Sept. 20

I always arrive at Redskins Park a little early to meet with Coach Allen in what he calls his "generals" meeting. The generals are guys he feels are in charge on the field. Besides me, the generals include Chris Hanburger, Myron Pottios, Richie Petitbon, and Jack Pardee. We go over strategy together every day for each game.

Coach Allen was still bubbling over our victory against the Vikings. He was especially pleased with the strong showing of the specialty teams. However, he pointed out the many mistakes we made as a team and we all agreed we must play better to beat St. Louis. The Vikings rolled up quite a bit of yardage against us, and we knew we had to tighten up our defense.

St. Louis is a good club with the potential to give us a hard time. They have one of the best tight ends around in Jackie Smith, who will be my primary responsibility as strong safety if I play. Smith is a tough man who fights every inch of the way no matter what a defense does to him.

We're pretty sure they're going to start a "rookie" quarterback named Tim Van Galder. Although he's classified as a rookie, he's been with the Cardinals organization for several years. He had a great game beating Baltimore in Sunday's season opener, so we know he has talent. But he's still a rookie as far as game experience goes and we'll plan our defenses accordingly.

After the generals meeting, Allen spoke to the whole team congratulating everyone on a fine game. Then we had our intersquad awards presentation in which players pass out awards to teammates who did something special during the game. The MVP award went to Bill Malinchak.

Another coveted award is made each week by offensive tackle John Wilbur. As our resident wine connoisseur, he prides himself on his knowledge of wine, and chooses a bottle from his vast selection for the outstanding player of his choice. There is one hitch — only players 30 years old or over are eligible. This has caused quite a bit of griping from those of us under 30. John just tells us we're not old enough and he abides by his rule. For this week the winner was our center Len Hauss, who played a typically outstanding game against Minnesota.

Specialty team captain Speedy Duncan also gives a weekly award to outstanding members of the specialty squad. His award is generally a six pack of beer, and no one can match Speedy when it comes to building up a presentation. He carries on at length about how he's studied the films carefully several times before arriving at his conclusion, and gives everyone a laugh. This time he awarded a six pack to all specialty team members for the Vikings game.

After the awards and our individual meetings, Coach Allen gave us an unheard of surprise. He let us practice without pads for the first time ever. That was just his way of saying, "Nice game, men." We appreciated it and had a hustling practice. The psychology of Coach Allen's move was great: we were so happy about not having pads, the extra long running we did seemed like nothing at all.

After our workout, the defense held its daily extra meeting with Coach Allen, where we all broke down our opposing personnel and discussed their tendencies. Discovering tendencies in the other team is very important. We'll search for any tip-off we can find that will indicate what they're likely to do in a certain situation. We think we've found some that will help us against St. Louis.

Thursday, Sept. 21

I arrived at Redskins Park at 9:30 a.m. today which is earlier than usual. I had to see Chester Minter, the accountant of the Redskins. As the Redskins' player representative, I had to go over information on the players insurance forms, such as changes of address or of beneficiaries with Chester. It's one of my jobs to keep players aware of insurance benefits in addition to rules, pensions, and fringe benefits in general.

Contrary to what a lot of players think, being a player rep is no snap. There's a lot of paperwork involved which takes up a surprising amount of my time. Plus, like any player rep, I've got my neck stuck out where it can be easily chopped off by management. Player reps have a history of being traded or benched. In fact, on the Redskins we have Roy Jefferson, Speedy Duncan, Jack Pardee, John Wilbur and George Burman, all former player reps for other teams. The Redskins probably have the most open communication system of any team in the National Football League.

One thing about ballplayers: they're not the most responsible bunch when it comes to something like returning completed forms. I have to keep after them all the time to make sure I get the forms back. Plus, the players love to bitch about red tape. On the Redskins, the biggest grouch is Chris Hanburger. No matter what it is, he'll bitch about doing it. He and Mo Pottios were giving me a bad time today about their insurance forms. But I have a sure-fire method of shutting them up: all I do is threaten to nominate them for player rep next time elections are held. Just the thought of winning that election never fails to make them back off.

Although our practice was lively, Coach Allen keeps stressing the importance of being prepared for the Cardinals. He's a notorious worrier, and he wants to make sure we're always concerned about our next opponent.

Perhaps it's his worrying that makes Coach Allen so well prepared. Today at our afternoon defensive meeting, he pointed out some very small details we had overlooked yesterday. He prepares charts which show a team's tendencies for us to study. I think if a player on the opposing team had a hangnail, Coach Allen would know about it and figure out a way for us to exploit it.

For this game, we feel our primary job is to stop their receivers—especially Walker Gillette and Jackie Smith. As a strong safety, I figure if Smith can't catch the ball, he can't hurt me. So I know if I play I'm going to have to stay right on him.

Friday, Sept. 22

Coach Allen wasn't too pleased with today's practice. Everyone was hustling, but true concentration was missing. I think it was due to the Monday night game which has made it a short week. It's hard to believe that in one more day we'll be playing the Cardinals. Coach Allen always reminds us that a team's attitude in practice is reflected in a game. If we don't get rid of this laxity, we are going to have a hard time beating St. Louis. All it takes is one missed call or a little daydreaming to cost a team the game.

Every Friday night Patti and I go out either to a movie or shopping or to dinner; it's another superstition of mine. Tonight we went to see *Slaughterhouse 5,* the adaptation of Kurt

Vonnegut's novel which received favorable reviews from critics Jerry Smith and Mike Bragg. They were right; we enjoyed it a great deal.

Saturday, Sept. 23

We concentrated on specialty team work in our morning meeting today, as we do on most Saturdays. I'm on the specialty teams, but I don't meet with them during the week because of my generals meetings with Coach Allen, so Saturdays, I attend the special team meeting. *Any* player who misses any meeting without a valid excuse is subject to a fine between $25 to $100, depending on Coach Allen's mood. He figures that a player unconcerned about attending meetings is likely to be unconcerned about winning.

At the full team meeting on Saturdays, we always have an official present who has watched us practice all week. He keeps a record of our penalties throughout the week and reads them to us on Saturdays so we can see where we've been making our mistakes. It's amazing how in a week where our concentration has been off, the mistakes we've made during the week will show up in the game.

We all enjoy giving our official a hard time, but we recognize his value. He's a tall thin fellow I know only as "Stringbean," the nickname we've given him. For this week, he's happy with our performance.

Saturday workouts are short and relaxed for the most part. Players frequently bring their children to Saturday practice so the locker room is generally loaded with kids. Tom McVean, our equipment manager, always has some kind of work for them to do.

After practice I went home and relaxed by watching the college game on television. But college ball doesn't interest me much, and I fell asleep until my little girls discovered me.

The night before every home game the team is required to stay at the Marriott hotel in Dulles, Virginia. The coaches feel it's the best way to operate because we'll have fewer distractions. I like it because from the day before a game through the game itself, I'm a real grouch and I might as well be out of the house. Jerry is the same way. It is the emergence of the animal in man.

After checking into the hotel, we have meetings. Then the specialty team lineups are read by Coach Marv Levy. He reads down the list position-by-position and the man playing the position calls out his name.

If the man is required to report to an official, the man says "report" after his name. For example, Coach Levy might call "Left end," and Bill Malinchak would respond, "Malinchak, report." We then watched films of the St. Louis specialty teams in action again, another of those little extras that Coach Allen believes in.

I returned to the room and Jerry was on the phone, ordering our traditional hot fudge sundae. We've been having one the night before our game for about four years now. It sure tastes good going down.

Sunday, Sept. 24

Congressman Walter Fauntroy from the District of Columbia spoke at our vespers services today. Filling in for Tom Skinner, Fauntroy related the ups and downs of football to those of life, how people must pick themselves up even when knocked down hard.

He joined us for our pregame meal of steak, eggs, toast and honey, and juice. It's amazing how some guys can shovel the food away at those meals, while others, like myself, eat very little. I feel this way: when I'm hungry, I tend to be arrogant and mean and that's how I want to go into the game. Besides, even after seven years as a pro, I still get a little fluttery inside on game day.

Today when I checked out of the Marriott I read my bill of incidentals carefully. Jerry and I always play a little game — I try to charge things to his name and he tries to charge them to mine. Last week he hit me for a few bucks, but this week he played it straight.

I bummed a ride to the stadium with Charley Harraway, Larry Brown, and Harold McLinton. I always leave my own car at home and Patti drives it to RFK. On the way to the stadium we talked about the game and what we had to do to win. The closer we got to the stadium, the quieter the discussion became, and by the time we arrived, no one was talking.

In the parking lot, we were swarmed by children, some of whom have been hanging around the stadium for years without ever seeing a game. I don't always have a ticket to give away, but when I do I like to surprise someone who's there frequently. They're always yelling, "Hey, man, how 'bout a ticket?" When I said, "Sure, here you are," this time, the kid could hardly believe it.

Richie and Rosey started again today. Benchwarming certainly isn't my stock in trade. I'm used to a lot of action and being exhausted and hurting after a game. I imagine Sonny feels the same way right now. We both watched for three quarters as Billy Kilmer built up a 24-10 lead. I replaced Richie in the fourth quarter and played out the game, but it just wasn't the same as being in there all the way.

When I got in, I knew the Cardinals were going to be passing, yet I nearly cost us six points. I got over-anxious on a play and tried to intercept a pass to Jackie Smith. My timing was a little off and I missed the ball. Fortunately, he missed the ball too, so I was saved.

We were a little inconsistent again. We dominated the game early with Larry Brown running all over the place and Jerry grabbing two touchdown passes. The papers have been saying a lot about how Jerry's not catching many lately, but he's always there in the clutch. Larry set the all-time Redskin rushing record early in the first half. Amazingly, this is only his fourth year as a pro.

Our specialty teams got things rolling in the first quarter when Mike Bass picked up a blocked field goal attempt and ran it in for the score. There's where that little bit of added attention to special teams in practice pays off.

By the end of the first half, Van Galder, the rookie quarterback, was on the bench and Gary Cuozzo, the veteran, was in. If Cuozzo had been in from the start, we would have been in a little trouble. He came in and moved the Cardinals for a quick score in the third quarter and Walker Gillette, the Cards' fast wide receiver, dropped a sure touchdown pass. If Gillette had held onto the ball, the Cards would have been back in the game. Gillette had slipped behind our secondary and had clear sailing to the end zone. We all breathed a sigh of relief when that ball hit the ground.

Only one game ball was given, and it went to Larry Brown, who ran for over 150 yards. He was completely exhausted after the game, a feeling I really didn't play enough to savor with him.

My daughter Robin was with Patti waiting for me after the game. It was the first time Robin had seen her Daddy play in person. She ran out of the crowd yelling, "Daddy, Daddy!", wearing a huge button that said, "I Dig Big Brig" on it. She jumped onto my lap and dirtied my suit, but it was sure good to see her there. As we walked to the car, she said, "Daddy, you're silly."

"Why?" I asked, a little surprised.

"Because it's silly to play that game where everyone gets

knocked around," she explained. "Why do you do it?"

I believe in being honest with kids, so I responded, "For the love of the game and the money." And, you know, I think she understood.

We ended the day by going to the post-game party at the Statler Hilton which Coach Allen throws annually for players and their families after our first home game. I could not believe the spread — roast beef, ham, chicken a la king, shortcake, fruit. As much food as there was, it was all wolfed down eventually. It was quite a celebration. Even though I'm not playing as much as I'd like to, it's great being on a winning team.

Verlon "Bow-Wow" Biggs gets another quarterback; this time it's the Cardinals' Tim Van Galder.

The New England Patriots

Monday, Sept. 25

Even though we won yesterday, we're receiving a lot of bad comments from the press and the fans. They say our style of play is "boring." For years the Redskins were exciting losers, now we're boring winners. There's no question in my mind which I'd rather be.

Tuesday, Sept. 26

Today I arrived at practice a little early to pass out reminders that the National Football League Players Association meeting was being held in the afternoon. Executive director Ed Garvey spoke about some of the new proposals the NFLPA is bargaining for. Garvey has a formidable job, traveling around the country to meet with all 26 teams. Frequently he runs into harassment from owners and coaches, but he does one hell of a job for the players. Most of the players showed up at the meeting, where Ed explained why dues were raised from 200 dollars to 300 dollars per man, and discussed some new NFLPA programs. The Association is trying to stop the use of astro-turf this year. It's putting pressure on some parks that don't offer players protection on the field. For example, some stadium walls are close to the field and they are not padded. A player could hit a wall and be seriously injured. Other parks have low fences which players can easily fall over. Of course, the NFLPA is also involved in straightening out individual player grievances.

We began preparing for the New England Patriots who are a potentially explosive team with a history of winning when they're not supposed to. They upset the Atlanta Falcons last week, and with strong-armed Jim Plunkett and hard-running Carl Garrett, they could be difficult opponents. Plunkett likes to throw to his old Stanford teammate Randy Vataha, a very shifty receiver.

The team MVP award for the St. Louis game went to Larry Brown, and Rusty Tillman received a set of golf clubs from a sporting goods store for his special team play.

Practice today wasn't particularly lively, and Coach Allen wasn't happy. We have to pick things up quite a bit to be ready for the Patriots. We've won a couple in a row now and I think we're a little bit cocky. We have to bear down and win the games we're supposed to win. When you stop bearing down, you get knocked off.

Wednesday, Sept. 27

Since New England has an astro-turf field, we've been working out on our astro-turf field at Redskins Park. Coach Allen came right out and said today at our team meeting, "If we don't shape up soon we're going to go up to New England and get beat." So we seemed to go out and try harder today and we looked a little better. Whenever we practice on astro-turf, everyone seems extra tired. It tends to wear your legs out more than natural grass.

A new therapy device arrived today, a paraffin bath which trainer Joe Kuczo ordered. It helps work the soreness out of jammed fingers or bruised hands, and coats the sore spot with wax. All the players, including me, were taking turns playing around with it just like a bunch of curious kids around a new toy. Guys were letting the wax drip off their fingers and harden into Dracula hands. *Worse* than a bunch of kids, I guess.

I had a lot of fun razzing some youngsters at a Pop Warner Football League speaking engagement tonight. They had team pennants around the auditorium and I noticed they had the Cowboys over the Redskins. I told them, "It seems to me you people aren't thinking right. That Redskin pennant should be above that Cowboy pennant because you *know* the Redskins are number one this year." That brought a few cheers out of them.

When I returned home there was still time to keep a promise I had made to myself earlier in the day. I'm involved in the Big Brothers of the National Capital Area program, and I promised I'd call my little brother Nolan Cowens tonight. I've been Nolan's big brother for five years now and I suddenly realize he's grown up on me at sixteen. We have developed a great relationship. He's a good little athlete and quite a photographer as well.

Thursday, Sept. 28

Practice wasn't as sharp as yesterday; we're inconsistent. At our defensive meeting, Coach Allen again worried that we could be in for trouble Sunday. We're definitely having our ups and downs this week.

Friday, Sept. 29

Another lackluster practice. We continually made little mistakes that could cost us in a game. Stringbean, the official, was catching penalties right and left. Offsides, holding, backfield in motion — these things could kill us. We don't have "presence" during practice lately — nor awareness, nor concentration. We're playing for the money now and we can't afford any mistakes. Here's a game we're favored in and we have to win. Dallas has matched our two wins, so we can't afford to lose one.

Saturday, Sept. 30

Stringbean read off our penalties this morning at our team meeting before we left for the airport, and I thought he'd never stop. I know one thing — we've got to get our heads out of our tail ends quickly if we want to win this game.

After arriving in Boston and busing to Foxboro, Mass., I met Tom Skinner and ate dinner with him. He asked how things went this week and I tried to explain our situation. "It's always hard to pinpoint what's missing during a week like this," I said, "but it's just that we're not together. We didn't have that close family atmosphere." I know Tom will try to say things during his vespers sermon tomorrow to help out.

I sat around tonight waiting to hear from Ricky Harris, an ex-Redskin and a good friend of mine who is now free safety for New England. He never called, but an old college teammate of mine, Dolph Banks, called and asked for game tickets. I told him to call back and I'd let him know about the tickets, but he never did. Some nights are just like that.

Sunday, Oct. 1

Tom delivered a powerful talk at vespers today, as I expected. He told us how families must move together. No man can move and achieve on his own. I hoped it would sink into some players' heads.

I always catch the first bus to the stadium whether I'm starting or not. I like to arrive early, get taped, go over my assignments, and concentrate on my job — I've got to be prepared in case I'm called upon.

During early-birds practice I saw Ricky Harris at the opposite end of the field shagging punts. Then I noticed an airplane flying around overhead and it was toting a big streamer saying, "Ricky Harris Fan Club," so I know he must be loved up here. He's been doing a great job for them.

Even during our team calisthenics, we weren't the lively bunch we usually are and I started to get extremely worried. I tried talking things up and getting other guys psyched for the game, but there was general indifference.

Sure enough, the mistakes we made during the week showed up in the game. We had a lot of penalties called against us and our game performance was just as lethargic as our practices. We were unable to contain Plunkett, unable to dictate to their offense, and we wound up losing 24-23.

Plunkett and a rookie running back named Josh Ashton tore holes in our defense. Ashton had over 100 yards rushing and Plunkett hit for about 250 yards passing. They went over, around, and through us, and our defense couldn't even hold leads of 14-0 and 21-17. The Patriots put together three long touchdown drives and got a 40 yard field goal out of Charley Gogolak, whom they had activated just prior to the game. They were ready for us.

Yet, bad as we were, we almost won it in one of the most frantic endings ever. In fact, we had it tied with less than two minutes left in the game, but our place kicker, Curt Knight, was roughed on the play. That gave us a choice of a tie score or a first down with under two minutes to try and score a touchdown. We went for the touchdown and didn't get it. Curt then tried again to tie it, but this time his kick failed.

The Patriots took over the ball and we forced them to punt. Bill Malinchak broke through and blocked the punt. He and Bob Brunet chased the ball and Bob fell on it but his motion carried him just barely out of the end zone before he had complete possession. So we got a safety, good for two points.

We were still in it after the Patriots' free kick from their own twenty. With just a couple of seconds left on the clock, Curt Knight tried a 50 yard field goal which just missed, so the score wound up 24-23. It was a rough loss.

I'm dejected that we lost and that I didn't play except on specialty teams. Every competitor feels he can contribute something to a game.

Driving home from Redskins Park after our flight from Foxboro, I couldn't help feeling a little bitter. I did some serious wondering about whether or not I still want to play this game. I feel I should be playing more. My performance warrants it, and I want to be in that starting line-up.

Two good things salvaged this day somewhat. I saw Ricky Harris and his wife Joy after the game. They had been having some rough times and were separated, but now it looks like they're getting back together. They're a couple of good people, and that made me feel a little better.

The second good thing was that Dallas lost today to Green Bay, so we stayed in a tie for first place.

The Philadelphia Eagles (2)

Monday, Oct. 2

I woke up today asking myself again if I still want to play football. I firmly believe any ballplayer who plans on being in football all his life is making a big mistake. I'm involved in ExTen Associates, a mobile homes development business. We're involved in setting up leisure time resorts in different parts of the country. I've been interested in it since I lived in California near a mobile home site.

Instead of going into the office, I met with Jim Burns, the overall manager of our mobile home developments in the eastern area. We had to spend the day driving to our Crystal Beach, Md., and Northeast, Del., projects. The hours on the road gave me a lot of time to think. Jim could sense what was on my mind. He tried his best to keep me from thinking football by talking about business deals, problems, and prospects, but still I couldn't get my football situation out of my head. I can't help it; I just don't like sitting on the bench.

After about a twenty minute silence, Jim spoke up. "Young man," he said, "I know what's on your mind, but there's only one thing you can do — keep pushing. I've been watching you this season and you've been pushing all along. Don't stop now."

That little bit of advice perked me up and I said, "That's exactly what I'm going to do, Jim. I'm going to keep pushing."

I was asked this afternoon by the mayor of Northeast to talk to the local high school football team which has not won a game all year. I went to the team's practice and they showed defeat everywhere; even in the way they carried themselves. In the locker room I began talking to them by saying, "You've got to be able to get up when you're knocked down..." Don't I know!

Tuesday, Oct. 3

Coach Allen is a very bitter loser. At our generals meeting today, he said, "I could feel it coming on all week. I should have put more pressure on the team so we would iron out all the mistakes we were making. But that's history now. Now we have to go out and concentrate and pick up a big win against the Eagles."

We know the Eagles well. Receivers like Ben Hawkins and Harold Jackson can spoil anyone's plans. At our team meeting today, Coach Allen reiterated what he had said at the generals meeting. Then he added, "As a result of our loss, I'm going to have to do something I don't normally do. I'm going to make some personnel changes." I assumed he was going to announce Sonny would replace Billy at quarterback, the move all of Washington has been talking about. Coach Allen didn't announce the changes then, but during calisthenics he came up to me and said, "Brig, I want you to work with the first team as strong safety."

Sweet, sweet music to my ears! It's finally happened; I've won back my job and now it's up to me to keep it. I know Coach Allen doesn't think I'm big enough at 5 feet, 11 inches and 190 pounds to play strong safety, but I've done it for many of my six previous years and *I know* I can do it now. As far as size goes, a lot of it depends on heart, and I'm loaded with that.

For the remainder of practice, I was full of piss and vinegar.

Wednesday, Oct. 4

Things just don't seem to be going right for Coach Allen lately. He has repeatedly requested that reporters not divulge strategy changes observed during practice. Any number of details might give the opposition just what it needs to counter our game plan. Yet the Washington sportswriters wrote all about the personnel changes, which also included Sonny for Billy, Bill Brundige for Manny Sistrunk, and Mo Pottios for Harold McLinton. Allen is furious and has banned all sportswriters from practice.

Many sportswriters seem to be bent on making a reputation at any cost. A lot of times they wonder why players won't open up to them, but so often the writer seems to print what he wants to hear. Many times players are misquoted or their comments are misconstrued. Who can blame us, under such circumstances, for clamming up?

While I've never had any serious repercussions from being misquoted, it is still irritating to have a writer put words into my mouth. I'll read things attributed to me that I *know* I've never said. While it probably won't cost me my job, it's not exactly a comfortable feeling. It seems to me a writer should be able to communicate with the people he's writing about — he'll get a better story.

Football is such a highly competitive sport — the only thing that matters to any coach or team is winning. It is stupefying how many times a team's strategy can be revealed by something mentioned in a newspaper article. We use that kind of information, and I'm sure other clubs watch for it too. I don't think sportswriters believe the seriousness of this. Sure, they have families to support and jobs to do like we do, but I think the home town press should be more cautious about what strategy is revealed.

Today's practice was excellent, even though it was held in the pouring rain. We have definitely recovered from our pre-Patriots lethargy: the task before us is crystal clear. We need a good overall showing before our home crowd to prove our determination. If we keep our present mood, we're going to play one great game Sunday.

After workout today, a group of sportswriters were waiting outside Redskins Park for Coach Allen to comment on practice. So George obliged them, right there in the downpour. All the reporters were scribbling furiously while rain washed away everything they wrote. It was a funny scene, and Allen loved every minute of it.

At our late afternoon defensive meeting, we studied films — again, charts — again, tendencies — again, and graphs — again. Coach Allen stops at nothing when it comes to preparation. I'm going all out to review all I can about the Eagles. It will be my first regular season start this year, and I've got to be completely prepared mentally. I sometimes feel the studying and mental preparation which goes into football is greater than the physical strain.

Thursday, Oct. 5

After another good practice, I hustled home to pick up Patti. We went to an art show put on by an Oregon artist named Don Precthel, who specializes in Indian paintings.

Don is a friend of my teammate Jon Jaqua, a hard-nosed specialty teams player who is a knowledgeable amateur art critic as well.

Patti and I enjoy art and we both liked Don's work. So did the critics who viewed his paintings tonight. The show was held at the Rudy Agra gallery in Washington and this was the first time Rudy had seen all of Don's work. He was impressed, saying simply, "This guy is great." The works were indeed striking. Don's brush strokes are impeccable. One of his paintings is now hanging in my family room.

Patti and I then went to dinner at my teammate Mitch Johnson's house where John Wilbur, George Burman and their wives ate with us. It was a nice relaxing evening. Wilbur always provides a lot of laughs. Tonight his hang-up was that he has a couple of homosexuals living down the street from him. "What will we do when our daughter grows up?" he asked at one point.

John's wife, Carol, is intelligent and easy going, but she likes to put him on sometimes. She said, "John, if they're homosexuals, we won't have anything to worry about."

John persisted and said, "Well, it just bugs me."

Finally Carol couldn't resist. She looked at him and said, "John, I think you're a latent homosexual!"

With that John got flustered as we all laughed, and all he could say was, "Aw, go jump off a bridge."

Friday, Oct. 6

Defensive backs occupy an unusual place in football. We're among the best all-around athletes since our positions demand strength, speed, quickness, and intelligence on nearly every play. We must cover a receiver running a pre-planned pattern and tackle backs 30 or 40 pounds heavier than we are.

We are expected to shut out $80,000 receivers and neutralize $100,000 running backs. We're at a premium on most teams. Yet defensive backs are, on the average, the lowest paid group of players in football. In most cases a defensive back can do his steady job all year, and still not find himself in that high-paying bracket. The reason, of course, is that football, and more significantly the football fan, is offense-minded. If that high-priced receiver can burn that defensive back just once for a touchdown, he's the hero and the defensive back is the goat. The back may have eaten up that receiver on every other play of the game. But the fans will only remember that the back got beaten for a touchdown. Most newspaper pictures are of spectacular receptions; rarely are they of a spectacular play by a defensive back. Since the glamour is in the offensive show, it's the offense that gets the publicity — and the money.

One thing we *can* earn as defensive backs is respect on that field with hard-hitting, intelligent play. In other words, we can see to it that the offense earns its money.

Saturday, Oct. 7

In contrast with last week's practices, this week's have been virtually free of penalties. Coach Allen is very pleased. We had a short practice in the rain today, and again it was a good one. We all know what's at stake tomorrow.

I fell asleep at home during the college game again and had to hustle to get to the Dulles Marriott by the 7:30 p.m. check-in time.

At our meetings, we were reminded once again to keep the pressure on Reaves, the Eagles' rookie quarterback, and to keep their outside receivers blanketed. Then Jerry and I returned to the room and devoured our sundaes. He promptly fell asleep after his last spoonful of ice cream. I was counting on a good rest the night before my first starting assignment of the season, but it looked like my roommate's snoring was going to ruin it for me. He never used to snore, but he's 29 years old now and I think old age is causing his snoring to increase. If I tap him on the hand or call to him, he jumps and screams like someone's after him. Then I laugh so hard because I got him that I can't get to sleep before he starts snoring again. I may have to get rid of this old man. But then, I don't know if there's anyone else on the team who could put up with him.

Sunday, Oct. 8

I bummed a ride to the stadium with Chris Hanburger and Len Hauss. I was uptight and concentrating so hard that I didn't say a word the whole time. I just kept thinking about what I had to do in various situations, to prevent any surprises. I even went over fundamentals like tackling. "Wrap your arms around the ball carrier, put your head in his numbers, and think *through* him," I reminded myself. There would be no lack of preparedness on my part.

There are no fans anywhere like Redskin fans. All-forgiving even after our showing in Foxboro, they even cheered us during our early birds warm-ups. Today, of course, they were excitedly anticipating Sonny starting at quarterback. When the entire team came onto the field, we began our drills by slapping our hands together, and the whole stadium took up the clapping immediately. Just by looking at my teammates I could tell there was no way we'd leave the stadium defeated.

However, the Eagles played well against us and at the end of the first half it was 0-0. Sonny had three good drives stopped by interceptions, two of them made in the end zone by the Eagles' fine free safety, Bill Bradley. It was obvious that our whole team was pressing a little. The offense wasn't having any trouble moving the ball; they just weren't getting the points. On defense, we were getting a good rush and good coverage, and containing the Eagles pretty well.

Like the true pro he is, Sonny came right out and took the game to the Eagles in the second half. As soon as we got the ball in the third quarter, Sonny began mixing up plays and he burned the Eagles with two long passes, one to my roommate and the other to Charley Taylor, as part of an 80 yard drive. Larry Brown plunged over to break the ice and we went up 7-0.

That drive seemed to be the cure for us. Though we only scored one more TD for the day, on a Jurgensen 35 yarder to Roy Jefferson, we played good hard-hitting ball the rest of the day. Our specialty teams saved our shutout when Ted Vactor blocked a Tom Dempsey field goal in the fourth quarter.

Sweet victory was ours again and the locker room showed it. We all felt the 14-0 score didn't indicate how well we had played. Larry Brown and Ron McDole received game balls. Larry had his fourth straight 100 yards plus game. Ron led a defensive line charge that harassed Reaves all day and sacked him a few times.

As for me, I played a good game. I forced plays the way I'm supposed to and I covered well. I knocked one pass away from Gary Ballman in the end zone on the Eagles' best drive. However, I have no room to be complacent. I've got to improve every week to keep my job.

The St. Louis Cardinals (2)

Monday, Oct. 9

The head of my fan club, Bonnie Westley, works across from my office. Today she and several other employees were waiting in my office to greet me with a big "I Dig Big Brig" button. Jim Burns was there too, and everyone was exhilarated over our victory and my starting role. It's great to be back on top.

To say my roommate is unorganized is an understatement. He, Ted Vactor and I had a speaking engagement together tonight. When Jerry arrived, he looked a little flustered and I knew immediately what he had done. "How many speaking engagements do you have tonight?" I asked.

"Well, Brig," he responded rather sheepishly, "just one — that is, one in addition to this one."

We let Jerry give his talk first and then he excused himself and left for his other engagement.

Teddy did his Cosby routine and it cracked everyone up again. As usual, I was laughing the hardest and I've heard it many times.

Tuesday, Oct. 10

We'll be off to St. Louis this weekend. It's a big game for them; they're talking title and if they beat us, they'll be in the race for sure. We've got to make sure we're not looking past the Cards toward next Sunday's Dallas game.

Coach Allen reminded us that Gary Cuozzo looked pretty good last time out against us, so he'll probably start instead of Van Galder. We've got to stop Walker Gillette, Jackie Smith, and Donny Anderson or else the Cards can explode.

Wednesday, Oct. 11

At our team meeting today, John Wilbur was given a rather hard time by one of the coaches and he was in pretty bad humor when we went downstairs to dress for practice. Diron Talbert was riding him while we were going down the steps and kept it up in the locker room. So "Strange" reached into his lunch bag, took out a chicken salad sandwich, and rubbed it all over Talby's face. Talby was so surprised he couldn't react. He just sat there turning red, licking at the chicken salad while Strange walked back to his locker.

Practice went well today. Sonny looks better and better as the rust wears off.

Thursday, Oct. 12

Even though this is our second go-round this year with St. Louis, Coach Allen has discovered more of their habits. He keeps stressing how strong they can be in their own stadium. But we look prepared.

Every Thursday is weigh-in day and the "heavies" like Verlon, Ron McDole, and Mo Pottios were at practice early trying to sweat off those few pounds to make weigh-in without a fine. Different players have different routines for their last-ditch efforts to lose weight. Verlon tries to tamper with the scale. Ron soaks in the whirlpool. Mo hops into the whirlpool, then into the sauna, followed by a hot shower.

Once weigh-in is over, these guys dig into their lunch bags and eat away, putting the pounds right back on.

Friday, Oct. 13

Every day before we take to the field for practice we reach into our little brown bags for a quick lunch. That's right — *football players* brown bag it to work every day! When you're counting on a little sandwich and piece of fruit to fill that emptiness in the stomach, nothing is quite as distressing as discovering your lunch is gone. You see, on the Redskins, we live in fear of a notorious lunch thief known as "Dirty" Biggs.

Being a bachelor, Dirty has no one to fix a lunch each day, so naturally, he is almost always without a lunch of his own. Yet he always eats. He'll snoop around lockers sneakily checking out the kind of sandwich each man has. He remembers who has the sandwich he likes best and, nine times out of ten, that man is minus a sandwich at lunch time. Today I left my lunch safely, I thought, in my car. I slipped out to the car at lunch time only to discover that somehow Dirty Biggs had gotten there before me. Sure enough, in the locker room he was sitting there wolfing down the last bite of my lunch.

One man who isn't bothered anymore by Dirty is Ted Vactor. I asked Ted to share his secret with me. "I was desperate for a solution," Ted explained, "because one day I purposely brought two sandwiches — one for me and one for Dirty. I figured this would keep him down for awhile. Instead, he ate the sandwich I gave him and then he stole the one I was saving for myself and he ate that too. I was determined to find a way to stop him. I found out he won't eat peanut butter, fruit cocktail, or any sandwich that is squashed." With that, Ted held out a severely squashed sandwich in one hand and a can of fruit cocktail in the other, his very own lunch for the day.

Saturday, Oct. 14

After our meetings this morning we boarded our plane and flew into St. Louis. We all seem confident and well prepared. We should give the Cards a good game tomorrow. I'm satisfied we're not looking ahead to Dallas next week.

In our hotel room, I reviewed some material for the game. My main responsibility will be Jackie Smith. He's the best all around tight end I've faced over the years. He can block, run, move, and catch with the best of them at his position. When the Cardinals' passing game is on, he can be their most valuable receiver. I've got to stay on top of him.

Sunday, Oct. 15

As expected, Gary Cuozzo started at quarterback for the Cards. Early in the game, he was getting good protection and he hit receivers on a couple of good pass plays. But this was one of those games where we stopped St. Louis early when we had to and then gradually picked up momentum. In the first half our specialty teams pressured Jim Bakken, the Cards' field goal kicker, into missing two attempts. Meanwhile, Sonny was spectacular throwing six for six in the half. His performance, combined with good running by Larry Brown and Charley Harraway, gave us nearly 200 yards offense in the first half. We led 10-0 at half-time.

The Cards came out tough in the second half and got a field goal to make it 10-3. But then our defense, especially

Verlon Biggs and Pat Fischer, caught fire. We forced a couple of fumbles, and Pat and Mike Bass had interceptions to help break the game open. I almost had an interception, but I just plain dropped the ball.

Our offense took advantage of the take-aways and converted them into scores. Sonny had us moving methodically, using a variety of pass patterns and taking advantage of Larry's fifth 100-yard-plus performance. He's unbelievable. Midway through the fourth quarter, Charley Harraway plowed over from four yards out to make it 26-3 and Coach Allen took out the first string offense the next time we had the ball.

Our second team offense could easily be a first team on many other ball clubs. Bill Kilmer is the quarterback, Bob Brunet and George Nock are the runners, and Cliff McNeil replaces Charley Taylor at split end. Now those guys are all seasoned veterans. They were in no mood for running out the clock, so Billy mixed up his plays and marched them in for a score making it 33-3. That's how it finally ended, with us looking stronger as the game went on. It's good knowing we have St. Louis behind us for this year.

Mike Bass gets ready to show his fancy footwork after his interception against New England.

Frustration was the word against the Patriots as expressed here by George Burman.

A cool Sonny Jurgensen returns to action against Philly.

John Wilbur (60) and Paul Laaveg (73) lead blocking for Charley Harraway around end against the Eagles.

Roy Jefferson and Charley Taylor trade some skin after Roy hauled in a 35 yard TD from Sonny to seal victory over Philadelphia.

Dancing Bear McDole grabs a handful of Cardinal Donny Anderson's face and Bill Brundige prepares to join in.

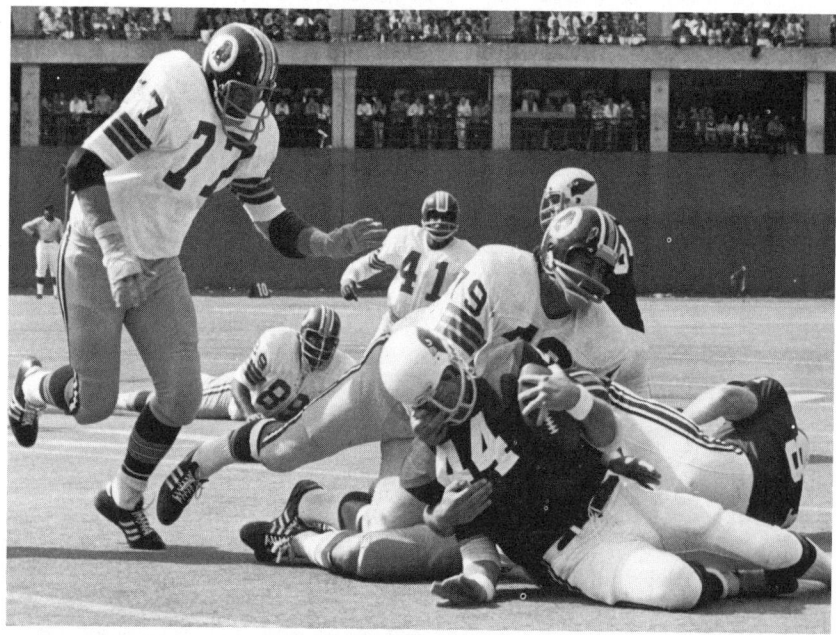

The Dallas Cowboys (1)

Tuesday, Oct. 16

This is the beginning of Dallas Cowboys week. We're all looking forward to playing those world champs. It was *snowing* this morning on the way to practice. The weatherman said it's the first snow this early in the D.C. area since around 1890. It looked more like Minnesota than Washington!

Coach Allen was quite pleased with our St. Louis victory, and he is bursting with excitement over the upcoming Dallas game. I doubt if he's even slept much, he's so wrapped up in it. He's obviously been preparing a great deal already, because his first words about Dallas were, "We can beat those Cowboys;" then he started breaking down their tendencies. We spent a good half hour in our generals meeting discussing some preliminary ideas about how to mount a defense against them. We must remember not to let all their shifting bother us. The Cowboys must have close to 50 offensive formations they can throw at us. We have to play *our* game and dictate to them.

The Cowboys are loaded with personnel. They are capable of scoring from anywhere on the field. Calvin Hill can run and catch — he leads their team in both categories. They have outside receiving strength in Bob Hayes, Lance Alworth and Ron Sellers and at tight end they can choose between two big veterans, Billy Truax or Mike Ditka.

But for all their talent, when I see how thoroughly Coach Allen has them analyzed, I know we can beat them.

Our good spirits were apparent at our weekly awards "ceremony" (as ceremonious an atmosphere as a locker room filled with half-dressed football players can provide). Pat Fischer received the MVP for his play against his old Cardinal teammates and he received the usual cheers and applause. From there on the awards got funnier and funnier.

John Wilbur was waiting for Coach Allen to call for his presentation and I happened to look at him. Strange takes the presentation very seriously and he was sitting there in great anticipation like a little kid waiting for his turn at show-and-tell. He's a perfect straight man, and he got up with all the dignity in the world and gave the wine to Sonny. John added this caveat, "Remember, this is to be consumed at your home and nowhere else," in reference to a recent "driving while under the influence" charge against Sonny which he is contesting in court.

Then it was Ron McDole's turn. Ron announced the winner of the Gator Award, an award which has an interesting history. At summer camp during Carlisle Fair time, Coach Allen gave Manny Sistrunk some money with the order to "win something for the team." Well, Manny spent all the money without winning anything so a sympathetic cashier gave him a gator. Hence the award has come to be our own Dubious Achievement trophy. Anyway, Ron made his announcement sound like an Academy Award presentation. He said, "The envelope, please," and he was handed an envelope. He opened it and continued, "The winner of this week's Gator

Award for his outstanding contribution to *practice* is.... Sam Wyche." The applause was deafening.

A special one-time award was made today and it was a classic. McDole's second presentation of the day, it was called The Chicken Salad Award, thought up by some creative mind last week. The award, graciously given to Diron Talbert, was a whole chicken between two huge slices of French bread with a stick of butter in the tail end. The entire team went hysterical laughing over that sight.

Coach Allen readily enjoys the team's humor, but he was anxious to get us prepared for Dallas. He's so excited about Dallas that he didn't even make us review all the films against St. Louis. We had watched about half a reel when he said, "Take those films off and let's look at those Dallas Cowboys."

His excitement is contagious — we would probably have been crazy enough to play the Cowboys today.

By the time we took the practice field, we had forgotten about the snow outside. Facing the miniature blizzard came as a rude shock. Equipment manager Tom McVean was on the astro-turf with a small plow pushing snow off the artificial grass. Speedy Duncan has spent a good deal of his life in the California sunshine and he hates cold weather of any sort. He took one step outside and headed back in, re-emerging completely bundled in about 20 pounds of sweat clothes.

Despite the weather, practice was very lively: Our attitude and spirit is great. We all sense our club is on the right track again. I can tell we'll be ready for the Cowboys.

Wednesday, Oct. 18

After every game, each player is given a form on the team we've just played. We evaluate the opposition as a team and individually, and write down our man's best moves and what we did to counter them. I handed mine in on the Cardinals today, and I noted that although Jackie Smith didn't hurt us this year, he's still one of the toughest tight ends around.

Coach Allen was bursting with enthusiasm again and he called the generals meeting five minutes earlier than usual. He told us that he'd found some *new* tendencies that hold up against Dallas. Then he shocked us by saying, "This is going to be the *simplest* game plan we've ever had." We just looked at one another and it was obvious we were all wondering how a team like Dallas could warrant a statement like that. Once Coach Allen explained things, we began to understand. Coach Allen's plan is for us *not* to match our defenses to their changing offensive sets. Most clubs, including us in the past, watch films of the Cowboys jumping around and try to devise special defenses for each formation. Coach Allen, who must know the Dallas films backwards and forwards, has discovered that despite all their shifting, the Cowboys only run a few basic plays from each formation. Therefore, we will just use our standard defenses and let them do all the shifting. Coach Allen is convinced that when the Cowboys go into their multiple sets but don't see us moving with them, it will confuse them. Of course, it keeps things simple for us too, which is to our advantage. I think it's a great plan, and I'm sure we can make it work.

Today's practice was excellent. We all know how important this game is and it's evident by our concentration this week.

Thursday, Oct. 19

Still raining. More astro-turf practice, a tiring ordeal especially on the legs.

Coach Allen has more acute information on the Cowboys.

It's fascinating how he can instill confidence. No matter how strong our opponents, he finds their points of weakness and convinces us of their vulnerability.

I could feel the concentration during practice, but a minor crisis is developing. Tom Skinner, our regular vespers speaker, may not be able to speak before the Dallas game. Coach Allen has a lot of respect for Tom and he was counting on him giving us that added touch of inspiration. I told Coach Allen, "It doesn't look like Tom's going to make it."

Coach Allen just looked at me for a minute, and then he said earnestly, "Brig, keep trying — he's got to make it. This is *Dallas!*" To understand how one man can be considered so indispensable, you have to hear Tom Skinner talk. Because he can move people, many players share Coach Allen's concern about his possible absence.

Friday, Oct. 20

Sunshine at last. We finally got to practice on real turf which seemed to pick us up even more.

Coach Allen's secretary left me a note saying Tom had called saying he definitely could not make it, but he would send Bill Panell, his vice president in his place. Call it stupid superstition if you wish, but the first thing that I thought of when I read Bill Panell's name was that he spoke to us in Chicago last year and before the Detroit exhibition this year. We lost both games. I know how crazy these superstitions sound, but I can't help feeling them.

This evening Patti and I went out for Mexican food with Mitch Johnson, his wife and another couple who were Mitch's friends. We somehow got on the subject of the 1968 riots, and I told the story of how my roommate and I were in the D.C. National Guard together at that time. Our unit was on the streets during the riots, and Jerry and I were given a station right in front of a *gun* store. I don't know what we would have done if someone had tried to get in, but I have the feeling we wouldn't have struggled. Neither of us is too brave and every now and then Jerry would look at me and say, "Rooms, this ain't too cool at all."

Saturday, Oct. 21

I brought a couple of little buddies of mine to practice with me today. They enjoyed seeing that a football player has to do more than just go out and play on Sunday.

Sully, our official at practice this week, said he never saw such concentration during a week of practice. We only had a couple of penalties.

At home, I feel asleep during the Oklahoma-Colorado game but not before seeing enough of Greg Pruitt to be convinced of his ability despite his size.

At our meetings tonight in the Marriott, Coach Allen was all over us, reminding us of every possible detail. He expressed his concern about Bill Panell to me through an assistant coach. "George is worried because of Bill's record against the Bears and Lions," I was told.

"Tell him not to worry," I said. "Bill's here now and he'll do the job."

Just then Coach Allen came around the corner and we went through it all again. He wants everything to be perfect for this one.

Sunday, Oct. 22

Jerry was up and out to church even before I awoke at 8:00 a.m. I had planned on sleeping until 8:45 or so since our game isn't until 4:00 p.m. today. But I couldn't go back to sleep. I was itching so for this game.

I ate breakfast with Bill Panell just prior to vespers. He went over some last minute items to include in his talk. "Just remember," I cautioned him, "keep everything positive; no negativism at all."

Coach Allen tells the story of a speaker who talked to the Rams once and kept mentioning injuries and possibilities of getting hurt. "The team was so shook during vespers," he recalls, "we went out and had a very unaggressive game."

Bill did a fantastic job at vespers, although only about 10 or 12 players attended, as opposed to the 30 or so who regularly show up for Tom Skinner. They missed a powerful talk. Coach Allen talked with Bill for a good fifteen minutes about his sermon. When I saw that, I knew there were three relieved men around — Coach Allen, Bill Panell and me. Of course, in order for Coach Allen to be completely convinced that Bill was no jinx, we'd still have to beat Dallas.

RFK Stadium was nearly full when I took the field at 3:15 p.m. with the rest of the early birds. Forty-five minutes before game time those great Washington fans were there to greet us. I saw a lot of old friends from my Dallas days — Cowboys owner Tex Schramm, Bill Bryant, Jerry Tubbs and others. I said to myself, "Hi, fellas. You're going to get your asses knocked off."

Nothing went our way early in the game and we had to come back twice from 13 points down — 13-0 and 20-7. We made mistakes, had some penalties go against us and just couldn't get untracked. It would have been worse if Calvin Hill hadn't dropped a Craig Morton pass with nothing but wide open spaces in front of him. Mo Pottios, our middle-linebacker, had the responsibility of covering Hill on that particular play, and he was pumping his legs furiously to catch Calvin, but there was no way. Calvin must have had his mind on taking that ball home before he had possession of it. Lucky for us.

We didn't get our game going until the second half, when Sonny and Larry Brown got our offense moving. Sonny mixed up his passes to our talented receivers, occasionally flipped one out to Larry, and we turned the game around. For the first time this year, Larry ran less than 100 yards, but he kept the Cowboys wondering where he would be coming from next. He picked up key first downs and simply refused to be held back. I could tell from the way we were hitting that we'd come back. And we did, finally winning it 24-20.

Football games can be turned around in a number of ways, but in this case it was sheer determination combined with hard hitting. I know I got in some of my best shots this year breaking up a couple of important third down plays. After the game, Coach Allen said, "The crowd was worth three points today." He wasn't exaggerating. The fans were so psyched, their screaming made the ground rumble. When Speedy Duncan made a key interception late in the fourth quarter, the entire place went crazy. We were a little excited ourselves.

Our locker room was filled with what Coach Lombardi would have described as "the joy and happiness of victory." When the noise finally subsided, none other than Bill Panell, the supposed jinx, led us in prayer. Then we sang our "horse's ass" chant four different times as game balls went to Sonny, Larry, Speedy, and our center, Len Hauss, who played with an injured leg although he missed almost all of practice the previous week. One bleak note — Bill Malinchak, our specialty teams standout, suffered a bad knee injury. He'll be out indefinitely.

It was one great day for the Redskins, but our schedule

makes every game a must if we are to win our division. We face the red-hot Giants in New York next Sunday, the Joe Namath Jets in New York two weeks from today, and the Giants again here in Washington in three weeks.

With a schedule like that, I'd better get some rest for now.

Dallas quarterback Craig Morton gets a good look at Chris Hanburger on a blitz as he releases a pass.

Roy, Charley, and Jerry—you won't find three better receivers on any other team in football.

Dallas' Calvin Hill thought there was running room, but Rosey (22), Mo Pottios (66), and Verlon (89) thought otherwise.

The New York Giants (1)

Monday, Oct. 23

Veterans Day. I got up early today to go to the Woodward & Lothrop warehouse to help kick off the United Givers Fund drive. People were enthralled with yesterday's victory. I stopped in at my office for a while, and then made it home to rest. My body is feeling some pain today.

Tuesday, Oct. 24

Although Coach Allen is still bubbling over our Dallas game, he begins to stress how we must prepare for the Giants, an explosive club this year. "Dallas is history now," he says. "Let's look at those Giants."

Norm Snead leads the NFC is passing and New Yorkers are talking title. Snead was acquired by New York in the deal that sent Fran Tarkenton to Minnesota. A lot of people screamed that the Giants were crazy, but so far they've been winning while the Vikings are having their troubles. New York has a great runner in Ron Johnson and he's also their leading receiver. Don Herrman, Bob Grim and Rich Huston are good wide receivers, and Bob Tucker, their tight end, led the league in pass receptions last year. The Giants can be dynamite! In a way, we're fortunate to play them right after Dallas, because the Giants use many of the same sets the Cowboys do. I think that's because so many Dallas coaches played for the Giants.

Larry and Sonny shared the MVP award for their outstanding game against Dallas. Larry also received the "offensive player of the week" award from the Associated Press. Sonny received Wilbur's wine; Mike Fanucci, a defensive lineman and one of the youngest Redskins, received the Gator, and Speedy bought a six pack for every member of the specialty teams.

Coach Allen pointed out an article in a New York paper which quoted some Giants as saying we were lucky to beat Dallas and that it would be a different story in New York. Our answer is to let them talk; games are decided on the field, not in the newspapers. No team likes to feel it was lucky to win, or won despite a bad game, but let's face it, a victory is a victory. In the standings, there's no asterisk saying "lucky win" or "played poorly, but won." They all count the same. Sure, New York will be tough in Yankee Stadium, but we're going to turn their fans against them.

Just when we began to suit up for practice, Coach Allen interrupted us. He said, "You fellas had a fine game, a hard game on Sunday, and we've got a tough one coming up. Let's take the rest of the day off."

Even the most zealous football player appreciates that after a game like Sunday's.

Since it was early, I stopped in at the motel where our team parties are held, and I talked with Manager Roy McKay about some business deals. Then I went home to spend some of my unexpected free time finishing up some work in my recreation room.

Wednesday, Oct. 25

Now the Cowboys are saying we were lucky. They can go ahead and talk. We're on top, and they have to catch up. I doubt if they will, at the rate we're going. All these comments are helping to get us psyched.

I don't think the average fan realizes how much preparation goes into one Sunday afternoon of football. We probe for patterns constantly. We feed information into a computer, look at game films, read past reports, discuss things among ourselves — anything to discover what the team's tendencies are. After we find them, we study so we're sure to remember them.

It was a lively, confident practice. We know the mission ahead of us. We want it all, but know we have to take one game at a time.

This evening I put in an appearance for the Leukemia Society at a Virginia shopping center. While I was signing autographs one young fella came up and said, "You know, the Cowboys should have won that game." Then he handed me a piece of paper to autograph. "Why should I sign this if you feel that way?" I asked, amused at his straightforward manner. He was taken aback. "Well," he finally said, "I'm a Cowboy fan, but you're my favorite Redskin." I said, "O.K. That's good enough for me," and I signed the paper.

I act as Coin-Boy Chairman for the Society every year. I'm active in it because my oldest brother died of cancer at the age of thirty. I feel one good way to help fight the disease is to go out and work for funds. In the course of my work I've become very close to a 12-year-old leukemia victim named Michael, one of the most determined individuals I've ever met. A couple of months ago I went to see him in the hospital when his condition was critical. The doctors didn't know if he'd pull through, but within a couple of weeks Mike was released from the hospital and out playing basketball. Like any good man, he got up when he was down. When you see kids in a leukemia ward, you realize how much a healthy person with healthy children should thank the Lord.

I went to see Mike at his house tonight after my appearance. He's doing well, and his spirits are good.

Thursday, Oct. 26

Coach Allen pointed out at our defensive meeting that we haven't been turning the ball over to our offense as often as last year. That's one of the areas we've got to improve on. We've got to force more fumbles and force the quarterbacks into throwing badly so we can get some interceptions. If we can set up our offense with good field positions, it'll make their job that much easier.

We had a very spirited workout. There's no let down in sight.

I hustled home in order to keep a date with my two little girls, for whom I'd promised to cut out a Halloween pumpkin tonight. Every year I buy them the biggest pumpkin I can find, and this year's is a record: it weighs in at just over 30 pounds. Unfortunately, when I got home, Robin and Tracy were in bed. I was disappointed because I get a big kick out of kids around a pumpkin or decorating a Christmas tree. Guess I'll squeeze it in tomorrow night.

Friday, Oct. 27

At breakfast today, Robin, who eats with me every morning, chided me for not being home in time to cut the pumpkin. "Now, Daddy," she said, "don't forget to come home right away tonight to cut the pumpkin for us." I told her I wouldn't forget and she reminded me right up until I left for practice.

Coach Allen pointed out how New York players, sportswriters, and fans are still talking. One of the writers said we'll be lucky to win half our games. From the looks of our workouts, the Giants better be prepared to back up all the talk. Past Redskin teams had some tough times against the Giants; for example, we once blew a three touchdown lead in the fourth quarter when Fran Tarkenton was their quarterback. Tarkenton still says that was one of his biggest thrills in football. I don't like the Giants much. They've always talked a lot.

We've been giving Verlon Biggs a hard time. He'll be playing across from Willie Young, and he and Willie always go at it. We're saying stuff like, "Hey, Verlon, Willie's going to chew you up," or "Here comes another long day for Verlon." Verlon doesn't say much — he'll answer on the field.

Right after our defensive meeting, I headed straight home. Despite what I told Robin, she and the pumpkin will have to wait until Patti and I get home from our Friday night out. Robin was very understanding. "O.K., Daddy," she said, "but you and Mommy be sure and come home right away. Tracy and I will be waiting for you." From the way I say "yes" to her, you'd think *I* was the child.

After going with Mitch Johnson to see the movie *Sounder,* a great family story, Patti and I went home to cut the pumpkin. As you might have guessed, Robin was waiting. "Get the pumpkin, Daddy," she demanded as we walked into the house. I did just what she said (who am I to argue?). Robin talked and Tracy babbled excitedly while I cut out a face. They were scooping out the insides and having a ball. When I cut out a fierce mouth and put a lighted candle in the pumpkin, however, it gave them both a little scare. Robin got over it quickly and began hugging and kissing the pumpkin, but not little Tracy. She just stood across the room and blew kisses at it with a worried expression on her face. I finally persuaded Tracy to get close enough for us to get a picture around the pumpkin, but she was still wary.

I put the pumpkin in the picture window, I'm sure it's going to scare some of the little trick-or-treaters. It's great to see people, especially kids, enjoying themselves over something like a pumpkin. Every kid should have the opportunity to have that kind of fun.

Saturday, Oct. 28

We arrived in the rain in Saddlebrook, New Jersey, this morning. Coach Allen dislikes New York and he keeps us a good 30 miles away from the city so no one is tempted in any way.

At 5:00 p.m. I met the sister-in-law of a friend in the lobby. She came to pick up some tickets I had for her. She's quite attractive, and while we were talking I noticed John Wilbur checking her out. John looked for a good forty-five minutes, and even came over and sat next to us. All the while I just ignored him pretending I'd never seen him before. Finally, my friend said, "Is that guy watching us? He looks like he's trying to get our attention."

I explained who he was, and then I figured we'd have some fun at Wilbur's expense. "Why don't I introduce you to him, and tell him you and I used to be engaged? I suggested. "Let's say that every time I'm in New York, we meet each other."

When John came back and we told him the story, he looked quite befuddled. He didn't know what to think. Later this evening, he asked me about her again, and I just played him on. What a character.

At our team meetings, Coach Allen again stressed what

we have to do to beat the Giants. We have momentum now, and we don't want to give it up. We've got to keep rolling. One thing's for sure — we're tired of hearing the Giants talk. The papers today are filled with the same comments we've been hearing all week. They've helped get us up for this game.

Sunday, Oct. 29

When the Giants came out after introductions, they were sky high. The New York crowd was going crazy and the Giants did not want to disappoint their fans.

It was one of those games where the action never lets up. Early in the first quarter, Sonny completed a pass to Roy Jefferson for a good gain. I was watching happily on the sidelines when suddenly I noticed Sonny limping toward the bench. He had good protection on the play and no one had hit him so we were all puzzled at first. As he ran on to take Sonny's place, Billy asked Sonny what had happened. Sonny just shook his head grimacing in pain and he hobbled to the sideline. We found out later it was a torn Achilles tendon. Sonny would be out for the year.

Billy rose to the occasion. After Jack Pardee recovered a ball I helped jar loose from Ron Johnson in the first quarter, Billy brought us into field goal range. With Sonny out, it meant I would hold on kicks. I was a little nervous, but Curt made it good and we led 3-0.

Later in the first quarter Sonny came over and said, "Brig, you realize that if anything happens to Billy, you'll have to quarterback. Do you know the plays?" He was right. Since I quarterbacked in college, I was the back-up quarterback with Sam Wyche on the cab squad. That shook me, but I started taking some snaps on the sidelines. I told Sonny, "If I go in there, I'm going to be drawing plays in the dirt. I'll give our ground game a workout." I was praying for Billy.

In the second quarter, with the score 3-3, Billy marched us down the field and hit Larry on a short touchdown pass. I fumbled the snap on the extra point try and Curt couldn't kick the ball. Part of my problem stemmed from worrying about the possibility of quarterbacking.

After I blew the extra point, I realized I couldn't let it affect my game and I settled down.

At half-time we were behind in statistics, but ahead 9-6 on the scoreboard where it counts. We were containing the Giants on the ground, but Snead was hitting on his passes. Still, they had only two field goals.

In the third quarter we came out and played very tough defense. Pat Fischer and I both narrowly missed interceptions. There was some fierce hitting and when the smoke cleared, the game was turned around by Chris Hanburger, who stole a ball right out of Ron Johnson's arms. On the next play Larry took off on a 40-yard touchdown run and we went up 15-9. I didn't fumble the snap and Curt's kick made it 16-9. Some of the Giant fans showed how bush they are when, after Larry's touchdown run, they threw beer on him. It takes more than a beer bath to stop Larry Brown.

We were never behind or tied again, winning it 23-16. Larry had yet another fantastic day, rolling up just under 200 yards in rushing alone. We felt great beating the Giants in their own back yard. Billy, who had to come in cold to direct our offense, received one game ball and Larry received the other.

We left New York right away, yet even before we left, we heard the Giants were still complaining that we were lucky. Some guys never stop bitching.

On the plane ride I talked to Sonny. He was a little down, naturally, but he said, "Brig, there's no way this is going to end my career. I'll be back." Sonny has the guts to do it.

It felt good to get home. I can't help thinking that bachelors on the team must be a little lonely after a tough game like ours. No one's at home to rub them down, cook a meal, or simply to talk with them. There just can't be that kind of companionship on the street.

After his finest start in years, Sonny suffers a setback with a torn Achilles tendon in Yankee Stadium.

The Over-the-Hill Gang will get their man somehow, as the Giants' Ron Johnson finds out.

Tom Skinner leads us in prayer, not for the Redskin victory over the Giants, but for the Redskin family.

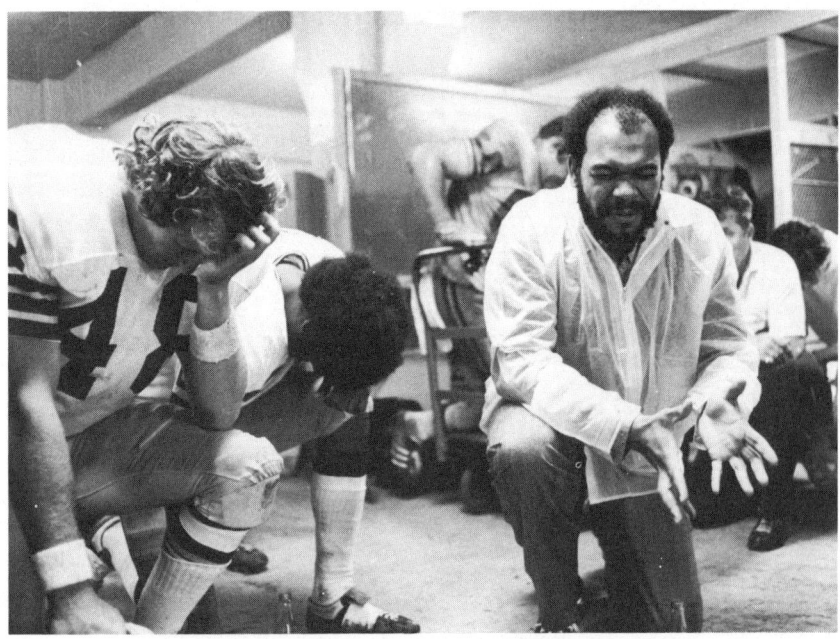

The New York Jets

Monday, Oct. 30

Len Hauss, Walter Rock, Tommy Mason and I flew down to Norfolk, Va. today to appear at some stores. Quick airplane flights never seem to go right. We were ready to take off when it was announced that our fuel gauge wasn't working. All the fuel had to be taken from the plane to see how much was in it, and then it had to be refilled. Then a flat tire had to be repaired. Walter "Zeke" Rock, always a wit on an airplane, wondered out loud if the pilot's compass was working.

It turned out to be an enjoyable flight, mainly since Zeke kept a steady flow of cracks coming. He drove the stewardess crazy. First he'd ask "What kind of drinks do you serve?" Then, "What kind of food do we get?" "Will you take American Express or Carte Blanche?"

We were just a little late, so we had to rush to our stores. I went downtown to an old Sears store, and there was a long line waiting when I got there. I started signing autographs and answering the usual questions. With the Jets coming up, the most popular question was "What do you think of Joe Namath?" My pat answer was a truthful one, "He's probably the best quarterback in football today."

One frequent question that always shocks me is, "Are you going to win Sunday?" People don't seem to realize that's like asking, "Are you breathing?" You have to believe you're going to win in this game, otherwise there is nothing.

The autograph session was fun. A lot of young people showed up, and I always enjoy them. When it was over, I met the rest of the guys for dinner and we hustled to the airport to catch some of the Dallas-Detroit game on television. Naturally, we were pulling for Detroit, but the Lions for some reason haven't been playing good ball. We never did get to see the game because the airport televisions were out of order. Dallas beat the Lions but it doesn't matter that much — we can't expect someone else to do our work for us.

When I got home, Patti reminded me that tonight was the team Halloween party. I didn't feel like going at 11:00 p.m., but she was ready with a big clown costume she had bought for me. She was wearing a devil's suit. So we went, and it was quite a scene. Everyone wore some kind of strange outfit. Talby and Jack Pardee came as gorillas, and they have the stomachs to play the part. George Burman was an Indian and he had his entire body painted. Ted Vactor came as a Mexican with a big sombrero and a blanket. His wife, Stacy, came as Ted Vactor. She's so tiny she wore her son Tory's Redskin outfit and Tory is only six years old! Jerry came as, get this, a priest. Roy Jefferson, dressed in a bright blue suit with wide lapels, was a pimp. His wife, Candy, was a dance hall girl. Mike Bragg came as Dracula, a remarkable likeness, and his wife Jan was Moms Mabely. Charley Taylor and Rosie Taylor were prisoners. Strange Wilbur made a suitable choice — a vagabond. The food and music were great. Ron McDole dressed as Oliver Hardy, and he looked just like him. We call

Ron the Dancing Bear because he loves it, and danced every number and with every woman in sight.

To cap the evening, I won some marble candleholders as a door prize. This party was a first in the Redskin organization, but it won't be the last.

Tuesday, Oct. 31

Everyone was tired today after our party. Coach Allen was brimming with enthusiasm over the Giants win, but he began to caution us immediately about our next opponent, the New York Jets. The Jets have been playing at their Super Bowl potential and they're right behind the undefeated Miami Dolphins. A victory over us will keep their momentum going and keep the pressure on Miami.

Wednesday, Nov. 1

Larry Brown was again our MVP for his performance against the Giants. He was also named the AP Offensive Player of the Week for the second week in a row — no one else has ever done that. Not only that, Larry earned himself a spot on the cover of *Sports Illustrated*, a rather dubious honor, as this magazine is infamous for jinxing athletes who appear on its cover. Guys have been kidding Larry about the jinx, but Coach Allen has taken it seriously. He called up the editors of *Sports Illustrated* and asked if Larry's picture could be removed before the magazine is published. He was politely turned down, and I'm sure he's a bundle of nerves over the situation.

Rusty Tillman presented a special award today. He gave

Mike Bass a baseball glove with his name on it, commemorating Mike's catch of the Giants' onsides kick in the last two minutes. Mike was in the line-up for Rusty because we were anticipating an onsides kick. Rusty, a linebacker, was very happy Mike was in his place.

Thursday, Nov. 2

Coach Allen feels the Jets may be the best offensive team we'll face. Joe Namath has the legendary Don Maynard, Eddie Bell and Rich Caster, all very fast receivers, to throw to, with John Riggins and Emerson Boozer providing a tough ground game. Bell and Caster run the hundred in two claps of a hand, and Maynard is a crafty veteran. Boozer has already scored twelve touchdowns. All in all, the Jets lead pro football in offense.

To control the Jets, we have to control their ground game. If Namath gets the ground game working, his passing will be unstoppable. We've got to mix our defenses and disguise our coverages to confuse him. Our defensive line has to pressure Namath because given any kind of extra time he'll hit those quick receivers. It's going to be a big, big test for us, but Coach Allen already has intricate preparations for Joe and the Jets.

Friday, Nov. 3

Verlon Biggs, Jimmie Jones, and George Nock are all former Jets and we've been giving them the business. Everyone loves to pick on Verlon; he just takes it in stride. Some of the Jets have badmouthed him, and he's just waiting for the chance to show the Jets they were wrong in trading him.

Saturday, Nov. 4

We are well prepared for the Jets. We have to be careful against Namath because he probably has more football intelligence than any quarterback in the game today. He's great at reading defenses, and he likes to "look off" defenders; that is, he'll look one way and turn and throw in the opposite direction. So Coach Allen has made us aware of the need to disguise our defenses against Namath. Because he is so quick, we can't blitz him. Instead, we'll concentrate on trying to fool Joe and his receivers. We'll line up in what looks like a standard defense and, when the play starts, shift into a totally different coverage. The next time he sees us in our standard defense, we may go with standard coverage. The third time, we may change to still another coverage. Such deception has been known to win games.

Tight end Rich Caster, my main responsibility, is an especially dangerous receiver because he is a strong deep threat. To keep Caster from getting deep, and to throw off the rhythm of the Jets pass patterns, a linebacker or cornerback will cut Caster down off the line of scrimmage. That will keep him off balance, slow him down, and, hopefully, it will cause him to start worrying about being hit and break his concentration. I also know I can't let Caster catch me covering him too close or else he'll turn and beat me deep. He's already got several inches and 35 pounds on me.

As for little Eddie Bell, we intend to punish him. He's small, so we've got to try and rattle him hard every time we can and make him think twice about catching the ball. Namath's other wide receiver, Don Maynard, is always dangerous. However, he's very close to a pass receiving record and thus may be preoccupied.

The Jets have two fine runners in Emerson Boozer and John Riggins, and both are primarily inside threats. Against most teams, they'd tear up the middle, so clubs try to devise ways to stop them. But we're going to play our standard defense since our line has been very effective in stopping inside runners. It will be a tough, strength-against-strength battle between Jet runners and our line.

As one final preparation, Coach Allen and the rest of us are continuing our attempts to work Verlon into a frenzy. Coach Allen keeps reminding him that Jets coach Weeb Ewbank didn't think enough of him to keep him around. Verlon's quiet, but ready to prove himself.

Tonight a local New York sportscaster inadvertently did us a favor. He interviewed a couple of Jets on his show and they badmouthed us a little. They said they were out to beat a bunch of old men. One of them said something about Verlon not being as good as people think. All I can say is, "Thanks a lot." If there was ever any doubt about us being mentally on target for this game, that show erased it.

Sunday, Nov. 5

For the first quarter, our game today looked like it would be a display of offense for both teams. Billy went onto the field after the kickoff and in five plays he took us in for a touchdown. The Jets made no attempt to hide the fact that they were keying on Larry. Everywhere he moved, eight or nine Jets were on top of him. So Billy started handing off to Charley Harraway and Charley kept the Jets honest. Then Billy unloaded a 40-yard bomb to Roy Jefferson and in less than three minutes we were up 7-0.

Later in the quarter Namath got his ground game moving and the Jets moved down the field on a 60-yard drive. Namath's first pass was a 20-yard completion to Don Maynard, setting up a short touchdown plunge by big John Riggins to make it 7-7.

In the second quarter we turned the game around, but not before the Jets jumped to a 10-7 lead. The Jets were so conscious of Larry Brown that they based their defensive strategy on stopping him. They apparently felt that no one else would hurt them. The Jets were dead wrong. Billy used Larry as a ploy and kept the Jets off balance. Then he fired another long touchdown pass, this one to Charley Taylor making it 14-10 with just a couple minutes remaining in the half. Namath came out throwing to try to get some points up before the half, but Chris Hanburger intercepted and ran it back for a touchdown. Namath didn't quit. He tried throwing again before the half ended and Chris picked off another one. We had a 21-10 lead, two interceptions, and a couple of sacks at half-time. We felt good, but we knew that Namath is great at playing catch-up ball.

In the third quarter, Harold McLinton intercepted Namath on the second play of the period. Then, despite the gang that was following him, Larry Brown ripped off a run of about 25 yards. He's unstoppable.

Neither team could get much going until late in the third quarter when Billy hit Larry with a little flare pass back on our own 11. Larry started running and evaded just about every Jet on the field. He showed them everything on that one play — moves, speed, power — and no one stopped him. He went 89 yards to make it 28-10.

By the fourth quarter, Namath was throwing on every play, but without much success. Then Speedy Duncan fumbled a punt and the Jets recovered on our 15 yard line. Namath threw a TD to Maynard and suddenly our lead was only 11 points with about 13 minutes left.

Our defense clamped down hard. We harassed Namath, knocked down his passes, sacked him and kept up the fierce pressure. Finally, with about three minutes left, Verlon Biggs and Bill Brundige got to Namath and sacked him. Namath fumbled the ball and none other than Verlon picked it up and ran in for a touchdown from 15 yards out. That was the crowning blow and a sweet bit of irony for ex-Jet Verlon. The game ended 35-17. For the second week in a row we had been badmouthed in New York only to come up and ruin the joy in Fun City.

It was a wide-grinning Verlon Biggs who accepted his game ball and the "horses ass" chant. Roy Jefferson and Billy Kilmer also received game balls for opening up the Jets' defense with a blistering passing attack. As Billy explained to reporters afterward, "The Jets felt that by containing Larry on the ground, they'd ruin our offense. They stacked the line against him. They gave me the long pass, so I took it. I'll take it any time."

So will I.

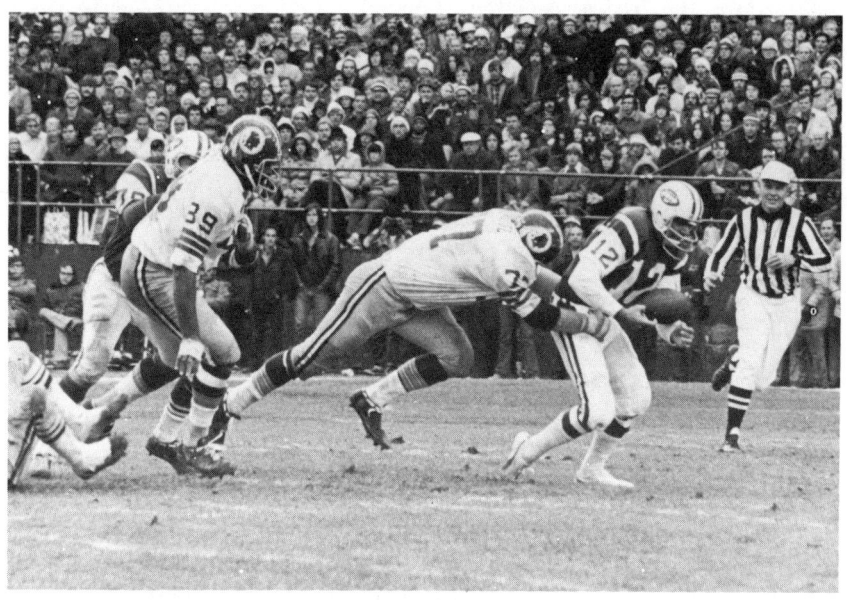

Joe Namath fumbles after being hit by Bill Brundige, and an obliging Verlon Biggs prepares to scoop it up and race for a touchdown.

The New York Giants (2)

Monday, Nov. 6

Not only am I feeling the soreness of our physical Jets game, but I feel the aches of the flu as well. While lying in bed today, I reviewed the Jets game in my own mind, and it dawned on me why all the CBS electricians had sly smirks on their faces when we walked into the locker room. They had, it turned out, cut the television wires so that people in Washington were unable to see the game. It's a shame because it was a great game to see. I'm still amazed at Larry Brown; he just can't be stopped.

I went to the doctor today to get some flu medicine and to also have my knee and neck checked out. I wrenched them yesterday and they were both sore today. I had a pinched neck nerve last year and there were times when my entire left arm went numb because of it. Fortunately, this time the doctor said I just need some rest. I'm determined not to miss any time; I've fought too hard this year to lose my starting position because of a flu bug.

I had a speaking engagement tonight and I was unable to get a replacement for it. I hate to let kids down when they're depending on me to show up at a banquet. They're the ones that make a football player a celebrity — they yell in the stands, ask for my picture, buy jersey number 23 at the stores, write letters. I can't let them down.

The banquet was at a synagogue and it was a nice affair. One particular incident made the whole night worthwhile. There were a couple of kids about eight or nine years old waiting in line for their food and they were trying to figure out which person at the head table was Brig Owens. Now, mine was the only black face in the place. So one boy said to the other, "Brig Owens is the guy with the black *hair*." That told me something about that boy's upbringing and it made me feel good.

Tuesday, Nov. 7

I got to practice early today to get some treatment on my neck and knee. Yesterday's rest helped my flu quite a bit.

At our team meeting, Coach Allen commended us on our victory over the Jets. He told us, "This win is a big step toward a division championship." He was pleased to quote Joe Namath's comment that no team's defenses were as difficult to attack as ours. We really did baffle Joe, but he showed his class. Instead of crying that we were lucky, he gave us credit and said he hoped he'd be seeing us again this year, presumably in the Super Bowl.

Awards were given to Larry today from a local radio station and grocery chain for his outstanding play so far this year. Speedy's specialty teams six pack awards went to Rusty Tillman, Jon Jaqua, Ted Vactor, and Mike Fanucci. Billy and Walt Rock received bottles of wine. The Gator Award went to Ray Schoenke for his activity in the game which consisted of getting knocked over while watching a kickoff return from the sidelines. Ray saw the play coming, but he just froze — and wound up on his back.

Coach Allen made us aware that we are going to have to work hard to get ourselves up for this week's Giants game. We're coming off a big win and we can't afford any let-down. The Giants don't respect us too much despite our win over them, and they'll be eager to beat us in front of our home crowd. We were expecting a workout today, but Coach Allen gave us the day off and my body sighed with relief.

Wednesday, Nov. 8

All worries about a let-down were erased today by some loud-mouthed Giants. Although we beat them in Yankee Stadium little more than a week ago, they are popping off again about what they're going to do to us. Jim Garrett, their defensive coach, has guaranteed that New York will win and that Larry Brown will be kept under 100 yards rushing. Garrett claims we were lucky to catch the Giants in the wrong defenses last time, but that it won't happen again. Even Giant *rookies*, guys who only have a few quarters worth of playing time, are running off at the mouth. To a man, we feel the Giants would be better off keeping quiet. All they're doing is giving us ammunition, and some have even given away parts of their game plan. But then, some teams, like the Giants, make alibis, while others, like the Redskins, produce victories on the field.

Coach Allen, the master psychologist, has a ton of clippings posted for us to read. There's no way the Giants will beat us in RFK Stadium this Sunday. They are making a grudge game out of it.

It was bitter cold today with a 40 mile-an-hour wind whipping across the practice field. The wind was so powerful it blew down the 70 foot tower our photographer, Nate Fine, takes pictures from. The wind seemed to pick the tower up and dump it over on its side. Nate had begun to climb the tower moments earlier but fortunately returned to the locker room to pick up something he had forgotten. In the time he was gone, the tower went over. Had he been on the tower, he probably would have been killed. The players were practicing on the astro-turf and the tower landed on the grass field. Had we been on the grass, it would have been a tragedy. We told Nate he should ask for flight pay or hazardous duty pay. Someone promised to bring him a parachute.

One good thing did come of the tower incident. A lot of the players used to lean on the tower and hang around it during practice; we won't be seeing much of that any more.

Despite the bad weather and the tower, we had a good workout thanks to the Giants' mouths.

I had a speaking engagement tonight at a church in Bethesda, Md. It was supposed to begin at 7:30 p.m. and I was late leaving home. Whenever you're in a hurry, problems seem to arise. I rushed to what I thought was the church and I saw a parking lot full of cars, so I assumed I was in the right place. Much to my surprise, however, when I walked into the church, I walked right into a choir practice. Then I noticed a banquet room downstairs, so I walked down and into a room full of elderly people who had *not* requested a football player to speak at their function. Finally, someone told me that, yes, there was another church by the same name nearby. More than a little embarrassed, I got directions and hustled off.

When I did arrive at the correct church, I was a few minutes late, but no one seemed to mind. Whenever I speak at a banquet, I can't help noticing how very nice people are. It makes me wonder why people can't always communicate on such a pleasant level. If people would carry their pleasantness into their daily routine, they'd do a lot for spreading communication and togetherness throughout this country.

Thursday, Nov. 9

I put my neck in traction this morning to ease some of the soreness out. I'm taking every precaution against reinjuring my nerve.

Coach Allen was still fired up as the Giants continue to talk about us. Their comments are getting very old as far as we're concerned. The one thing Coach Allen is stressing more this game against the Giants than last time is for us to be more physical. The Giants are really psyched, so we must hit extra hard from the start to show them we're in control.

As for personnel, Ron Johnson is their major threat. He's a strong runner, inside and outside and he's also the Giants' leading pass receiver. To stop Johnson, we just have to remember the fundamentals of tackling. Johnson must be hit squarely; he has such great balance, he'll slide off a tackle that isn't square and solid. He's a tough man to take off his feet.

Johnson's running mate, Charlie Evans, who is a great blocker, will miss the game because of a broken leg. That's a plus for us, especially since his replacement is a rookie from Nebraska named Joe Orduna. The rookie has had some unkind words for us, so we're looking forward to initiating him into pro ball.

My main responsibility is Bob Tucker, the Giants' tight end. Tucker is a good short pass receiver and runs well after making a catch. I can't play Tucker too deep because that would give him too much running room after his receptions. So I have to stay close to him and, if he does catch a pass, I have to bring him down right away. It's the opposite of what I used against the Jets' Rich Caster whom I covered deep to prevent the bomb at the risk of giving up the short pass. Tucker's running and short receiving ability mean a closer coverage.

It was another tiring astro-turf practice today since it was so cold and rainy. Only fools or football players would be out today — I guess we're both.

I got home to some free time tonight and spent it cleaning out my personal get-away room. It's one of those places where you put all your old notes, bills, magazines, clippings, and so forth, and only clean at long intervals. Tonight I attacked it. What a job!

Friday, Nov. 10

We've noticed the Giants are using fewer offensive sets lately. They're getting back to more basic football. Of course, they could be setting us up, but they're a strong offensive team even without the variety of formations.

I've said many times that Coach Allen takes every precaution in preparing us. Today he showed us some plays the Giants ran four or five years ago so we won't be surprised if they run them this Sunday. Sometimes he must get a feeling that a team is going to resort to some of its old plays. The canisters he got these films from must have had ten inches of dust on them.

We got a special report today from ex-Giant Clifton McNeil at our afternoon defensive meeting. Cliff refreshed our memories about the habits of various Giant receivers and mentioned a few we hadn't covered. Tommy Mason gave us a special summary on the tendencies of Giant running backs. We leave nothing to chance.

The sunshine allowed us to practice on the grass field today and we were livelier and sharper than usual. We intend to make those Giants eat their words.

Chris Hanburger, team grouch, was giving Double-O

Boynton a bad time today. He chased him and wrapped him up in tape. When Double-O got free and tried to escape on his bike, Chris fired a ball at him and dented his fender a little. That made Chris, whose bite isn't nearly as bad as his bark, feel bad so he helped Double-O straighten it out.

Saturday, Nov. 11

This afternoon after practice Tom Skinner and I went to visit Sonny at Georgetown Hospital. Getting in to see him was like trying to see the president. There's even a guard at Sonny's door since some newsmen and photographers tried to sneak in and get some pictures and stories. The room was loaded with flowers and bottles of wine. I brought him a roll of cashier's tape which workers in a nearby shopping center filled with signatures and get-well wishes. Sonny seemed slightly awed at all the tokens of good luck he has received and his spirits were pretty high.

Tom and I spent about an hour and a half with Sonny, talking and testing some of the wine. Sonny couldn't get off the upcoming game. He's having this Sunday's Giant game piped into his room via closed circuit. "Are you guys ready for the Giants?" he asked. "They're not going to be easy to get up for, especially since we beat them two weeks ago." He's all football, and before Tom and I left he told us there was no way this injury would end his career.

Sunday, Nov. 12

Tom and I caught a ride to the stadium with Charley Harraway. It was the first time this year that Charley had his car to drive to the stadium and he was quite cocky about it. "I suppose you two are in need of a ride again," he said to Tom and me. "Well, I guess you can have a ride with me — this week."

This was the game the Giants had guaranteed their fans they would win, the game in which Larry Brown would not gain a hundred yards. This was the game in which the Giants achieved neither of their goals. We won the game 27-13 and Larry had about 120 yards, but it wasn't easy.

It took our offense most of the first half to get untracked. The Giants had definitely come to play, and they drove in for one score as Norm Snead mixed up his passing and running game very well. Finally, late in the half, Billy hit Jerry with a touchdown pass but Curt Knight's extra point attempt was blocked. Then Billy got us within field goal range with about ten seconds left, but Curt missed the kick. We went into the locker room losing 7-6 and having to kick off to the Giants in the second half.

The second half kickoff was the turning point of the game. The Giants tried an old trick, a reverse on the kickoff, and we were almost caught. Rocky Thompson caught the ball, started running one way, and then handed off to speedster Eldrige Small who came racing in my direction. I was the only Redskin in front of the play and it seemed about half the Giant team took shots at me. Somehow, I stayed on my feet and caught Small's ankle on our 15 yard line. He went down and it seemed to fire us up. We held the Giants to a field goal, and, although we were down 10-6, we were ready to come alive.

It was Larry Brown who awoke our offense. With third and inches at midfield, Larry broke off a 35 yard gain. Then, with the Giants trying to hold us on fourth and inches at their five, he broke through for two yards. Charley Harraway put it over on the next play. We took a 13-10 lead when Knight made the extra point, though it was partially blocked. The Giants tied us at 13-all with about four minutes left in the fourth quarter, but Billy just marched our offense down the field and Larry scored with a little less than one minute to play. Curt's extra point was almost blocked again, but it squibbed over to make it 20-13.

At this point in the game, some of the fans started to leave. Those who did, missed a lot of fireworks. Ted Vactor intercepted a desperation pass and ran the ball back to the Giant 10. Everyone assumed we would just let the clock run out with 20 seconds left. Instead, one of our linemen told Billy that he had heard a public address announcement saying Larry needed only one yard to reach the thousand yard mark for the season, so Billy called time out. On the next play, Larry scored from five yards out and the Giants started bitching that we were rubbing it in, because, as it turned out, Larry was a good nine yards short of the thousand yard mark.

I guess the Giants were pretty hot, and after the extra point which made it 27-13 and ended the game, a couple of fights broke out. Rusty Tillman and John Wilbur were working as a tag team on a couple of Giants, but the main event involved our reserve quarterback and kick holder, Sam Wyche, and Giants cornerback Pete Athas, one of the players who had badmouthed us during the week. It started when Athas came across to block the extra point, as he had been doing all day, and took a late swipe at Sam. Sam, who is usually unflappable, really went after Pete. He was swinging away, but only with his left hand so he wouldn't hurt his throwing hand!

After the Athas-Wyche swing-out, which seemed to go to Sam on points, Ralph Hawkins, our linebacker coach, and Jim Garrett, the Giants defensive coach who had promised victory, had a shoving match. Giants safety, Richmond Flowers, jumped in and all of a sudden Coach Allen's 16-year-old son, Bruce, hopped all over Flowers. All this was happening right around me, so I finally separated Bruce and Richmond and things started to calm down.

It was a happy post-game locker room. Just as we had planned, the Giants went home moaning. Game balls and "horses ass" chants went to Roy "Sweet Pea" Jefferson, Larry, Tom Skinner, and Mr. Clutch, Jerry.

My roomo, Jerry Smith, accepts congratulations from Sweet-Pea Jefferson (left) and Mack Alston after being awarded game ball against Giants.

The Atlanta Falcons

Monday, Nov. 13

I spent a good deal of time today reflecting on that sweet victory over the Giants. We made them eat a little crow after all their talking.

This afternoon John Wilbur, Sam Wyche and I went as guests to a luncheon sponsored by Chris Hanburger and Pat Fischer. Sam drew a lot of attention from the audience because of his fist fight with Pete Athas. Sam revealed that Pete said at the end, "I don't want to fight you, Sam. I know your brother, Bubba." Sam, who admitted being furious, replied, "What kind of comment is that? What does that have to do with it?" The fight ended before Pete could answer. The fight made Sam a celebrity for the time being, but it's not the kind of notoriety he wants.

This evening I spoke at an assembly at Episcopal High School, a private boys' school in Virginia. This school has some unbelievable athletic facilities. When Coach Allen first came to Washington, he held a six day workout session in early spring using the Episcopal facilities. Some fine young men attend that school, and I enjoyed conversing with them. They have great ideas, not just for themselves, but for the country as well.

Tuesday, Nov. 14

We had meetings today, but no workout.

Coach Allen is still being blamed by the Giants for calling time out at the end of the game so Larry could score the extra touchdown. A couple of Giants have even gone so far as to imply that we were trying to beat the point spread, which was something like nine points. A team that talks as much as the Giants asks to have it rubbed in.

Earlier in the season, people were talking about how easy our schedule would be this year. Some of these teams (for example, the Jets, the Giants, and New England) may not have been much last year, but we've faced them at their peak this year. Our upcoming opponent, Atlanta, is no exception. In the thick of things in the Western Division, they're fighting for first place with San Francisco and Los Angeles.

Larry Brown, Roy Jefferson, and Jerry Smith received "most valuable" awards for the Giant game. Ted Vactor received a six pack from Speed-o, and Pat Fischer, who has been great all year, picked up Wilbur's wine award.

Coach Allen gave a special award to Clifton McNeil. It was a can of "mints" and he told Cliff to hand them out to his old Giant teammates if he went out to dinner with them anytime soon. When Cliff opened the can, a huge spring shot out and he bobbled the can. A great receiver who hasn't seen much action at all this year behind Charley Taylor and Roy Jefferson, Cliff said, "I don't really know how to handle this can, you know, I've been sitting on the bench for so long." I think that was his way of saying, "Coach, get me off the bench just a little bit, won't you?"

I went to an engagement tonight where Warner Wolf, the popular Washington sportscaster, was also a guest speaker.

Warner is usually great at these affairs, but the people attending the affair were so rude that neither Warner nor I could get comfortable. In fact, we agreed it was probably the most unruly group we had ever been asked to talk to. People kept shouting questions to me and remarks at Warner, and there was no organization. Many of the adults were worse than the youngsters, and had it been only a group of adults I would have walked out.

One little fella, about ten years old, came up to me afterwards and said, "I'm sorry it was so noisy. I didn't get to hear you much, so I hope I can hear you again some time." I talked to him alone for about ten minutes. It's the people who are interested who miss out the most when others are rude.

Wednesday, Nov. 15

We broke down the Falcons' offense and discussed strategy at our defensive generals meeting today. Atlanta, considered a breather by many people before the season started, is certainly no pushover now. They have a ball control offense led by Dave Hampton and Art Malone, two runners who grind out yardage with the best of them. Both Hampton and Malone are effective inside and outside, which makes them especially hard to stop. They are both among the NFC's top five running backs. The one weakness they seem to have is a tendency to fumble when hit hard. So that's our plan: another hard-hitting performance by our defensive line, hopefully causing some fumbles. No gimmicks; just strong, basic football.

Bob Berry, a Tarkenton type, quarterbacks the Atlanta offense. Berry likes to move around before he throws. He'll run with the ball occasionally, and he frequently sets up his passes with a quick sprint-out, stop, set, and throw. Berry has a strong arm and he can throw long, but he's not the most accurate passer around. We're going to harass Berry on his rollouts with some linebacker blitzes. We feel the blitz will surprise him and his protection and hurry him into some long, inaccurate passes.

Berry's most dangerous target, Jim Mitchell, is my responsibility. Coach Allen has called Mitchell "the finest tight end around." Mitchell's a real bull to bring down once he receives a pass. Since Mitchell runs short and long patterns equally well, I have to make sure he doesn't set me up for a bomb. He's deceptively fast, and so big that his speed isn't obvious until you get caught trying to match strides with him. He's a smooth runner with a long stride and he gradually overtakes defenders. We'll try to chop him down when we're expecting deep patterns, but there aren't many specific precautions to take against Mitchell. I just have to be ready for everything and not let him beat me deep.

We were one cold bunch of football players when we came in from our astro-turf field workout. There was a little snow and a little wind, and some of the guys were completely covered with sweat clothes. Pat Fischer even had a hood over his helmet.

A favorite lunch time dish around the locker room on these cold days is instant soup. The only problem is that you never know when the soup that was in your locker in the morning will be there in the afternoon. Today, because of the cold, there was an outbreak of soup thefts, and some of the players were saying, "What kind of family is this where people steal from one another?" Jack Pardee responded, "That all depends on the size family you come from." I know what he means: coming from a family of eleven children I learned early to protect what you can get your hands on. But the food thiefs on this team are something else!

Thursday, Nov. 16

Atlanta has great balance on offense and defense. We watched them on film today, and I think everyone realized how good they are because we went onto the astro-turf in the rain and had a strong workout.

Duke Zeibert, the Washington restaurateur, visited Redskins Park today, as he does every Thursday following a victory. He always brings an enormous victory cake with ice cream, and milk to wash it down. We enjoy kidding Duke about how terrible the cake looks, but everyone stands around stuffing it away. Somehow we always manage to eat the whole thing.

Friday, Nov. 17

The sun came out and warmed things up at last. We still had to practice on astro-turf though, since the natural grass was soggy. Everyone was turned on by the sunshine, and we had some lively drills. We look good.

I did some light weight lifting in our weight room today. I do this as the season goes along because I can feel the schedule taking its toll on my strength. Lifting builds me back up; I can't afford to lose anything as we come down the stretch.

Saturday, Nov. 18

Practice seemed strange today. Generally Saturdays are light, but since our game isn't until Monday this week, we followed our Friday schedule today. Everyone seemed foggy at first.

We finally got a chance to practice on God's green grass. It's a good thing, because that seemed to lift us out of our fog, and we had our best practice of the week.

When we got in from practice, Verlon started getting his daily barrage of phone calls. There's a phone in the locker room, and Verlon's girl must know when we step off that practice field. As soon as we come in the door, the phone rings. No one even bothers to ask who it's for; we just let Verlon go get it. So not only is he the leading food thief, he's also the top phone hog.

I must admit, Verlon surprised me today. His conscience must have gotten to him. He broke down and bought me a box of soups.

Sunday, Nov. 19

It seemed odd to practice today. My body seemed to be saying, "Hey, this is Sunday, game day. What are we doing out here?" I think everyone else felt the same way too; we've all become creatures of routine.

Coach Allen was not bothered by the odd schedule, however. He proceeded with our Saturday schedule right down the line. He reminded us that this coming Thursday, Thanksgiving Day, Dallas has a tough game against San Francisco. If we beat Atlanta Monday night, the pressure will be on the Cowboys to match our win.

Verlon light-fingered through today, stealing his first pack of soup out of the box he gave me yesterday.

We had our meetings at the Marriott tonight, and Coach Allen summed up what we must do to win. On defense, we've got to stop the running game. On offense, we must contain their excellent defensive ends, John Zook and Claude Humphrey, and middle linebacker Tommy Nobis. We'll use our usual offensive attack, with Larry running to set up Billy's passes to our fine receivers.

Tom Skinner joined Jerry and me for hot fudge sundaes. Jerry was in good form ordering the sundaes, saying "We'd like three hot fudge sundaes. Not those little things you serve in the restaurant. We'd like ours in soup bowls with three or four mounds of vanilla ice cream. Then trickle that hot fudge sauce all over the ice cream and just put a dab of whipped cream on top." They were beauties!

Monday, Nov. 20

We had a lot of time on our hands this morning. No one enjoys waiting around for these night games to start. Jerry and I ate a late breakfast together. Some guys went home and others called their wives, but I didn't do either. I'm poor company on game day, so I stay out of touch. I spent a lot of time reading and dozing in front of the tube until vespers at three o'clock. Then I caught a ride to RFK.

The locker room was quiet, as usual. When you hear noise in a locker room before a game, you're hearing the noise of a losing team.

Atlanta was formidable. Larry went over the thousand yard mark on his first carry of the night, but that was all we did right in the early going. The Falcons scared the hell out of us by jumping to a 10-0 lead by early in the second quarter. But then I started to feel something. We began to pull together, got ourselves settled, and then went to work on Atlanta.

Two turnovers, an interception and a fumbled punt, set up Atlanta's touchdown and field goal. Once we stopped making mistakes, we started clicking. Mike Bass picked off one of Berry's passes, but after a short drive, Curt Knight missed a 32 yard field goal. So we had to do it again on defense. Chris Hanburger pounced on a fumble at the Atlanta 37, and Billy came out and called an end-around to Charley Taylor which went to the four. Larry broke over and it was 10-7 at halftime.

On defense, we served Atlanta notice early in the third quarter that we were through fooling around. We held them on their first three offensive plays of the half. Our offense took over and finally started driving the Falcon defense out of the way. Billy made some great calls and climaxed a long drive with a short pass to Larry for a touchdown, making it 14-10.

We had the momentum, and our defense was fired up, particularly Ron McDole and Verlon Biggs. Then, with Atlanta deep in their own territory, someone hit Art Malone and the ball popped into the air right in front of me. I grabbed it, ran a few steps, and someone yanked me to the ground on the Falcon ten yard line. On the next play, Billy pitched a touchdown strike to Jerry whom we now call "Home-Run" Smith. He's got six touchdown receptions in 16 catches this year. We went out in front 21-10, and I had to feel good about my part in it.

We traded field goals in the fourth quarter and the game ended 24-13. In the fourth quarter, our defense swamped Berry almost every time he went to pass. Our front four had a great night, and we contained the Atlanta ground attack better than any other team has done this year. Larry was not contained however, getting about 80 yards. In addition to reaching his thousand for the year, he went over the four thousand yard mark for four years, a fantastic record. He got a game ball — the one he was toting when he went over the thousand yard mark. It was our seventh win in a row, the longest Redskin winning streak since 1945.

The Green Bay Packers (1)

Tuesday, Nov. 21

I thought we would have to go to practice today since we've got the Packers coming up at RFK this Sunday, but Coach Allen gave us the day off. We didn't even have to look at movies, a real surprise. We certainly need the time off to rest our bodies, but I don't know if we can afford to lose the preparation time. Each game looms bigger and bigger now.

I had a speaking engagement tonight, but I wasn't enthusiastic about it. As the season moves on, I want as few distractions as possible. We're on top, and I don't want anything to break my concentration.

Wednesday, Nov. 22

The crazy Washington weather came up with light snow for today. One day it's like springtime, the next day it's freezing. It must have something to do with the astronauts messing around on the moon.

We'll be facing another pair of big, fast running backs this Sunday, John Brockington and MacArthur Lane. Those two have brought the Pack back. The entire Packer team is big, young, and tough.

Coach Allen was pleased with our victory over Atlanta, but we're not going to be caught looking back on our past glory. Coach Allen pointed out that Green Bay is even better than Atlanta, offensively and defensively. One thing that he's wondering is why, with all their talent, the Packers put their offense in the hands of a second year man, Scott Hunter. Hunter relies on his coach, Bart Starr, to send in the plays from the bench. Starr was a great quarterback and the Packers may be running his plays, but it's not the same as having him in there running the team. Green Bay would be a lot better off with a more experienced quarterback.

Coach Allen has a few ideas about how to capitalize on Hunter's inexperience. Since Hunter is still new at reading defenses, and since his play selection is coming from the sidelines, we're going to be jumping into a five man line on occasion. Coach Allen feels that Hunter may have difficulty picking up the change. If he does pick it up, it will force him to check off at the line and perhaps force him into passing, which is just what we want. The five man line should cause Hunter plenty of problems. It also means Manny Sistrunk will see more action since his specialty is tearing up good runners. Manny is aching to get some licks in.

It is also part of our plan to force Brockington and Lane outside since they are both at their best on inside runs. At the same time, we've got to stop them quick when they do turn outside, before they get up too much steam. That's another burden for our line and linebackers.

As far as Green Bay's passing game goes, we are only concerned about one man — wide receiver Carroll Dale, a fast, strong, crafty veteran. His favorite play is an out-and-up pattern where he runs an out pattern toward the sideline and then turns up field. To stop this, we have to avoid overcommitting ourselves; when he runs his out pattern we must make sure that we're not so close that he's going to turn up field on us. It's tough to be that patient sometimes.

Coach Allen told a humorous story today. It seems that Monday night during halftime he went to tell the officials something. He walked into the room where they meet and caught them eating hamburgers! He thought that was incredible, and had a good laugh. Then he got serious and said to us, "You know, all food does is make you relax. They could get so relaxed they'd miss a call!"

Before going onto the practice field today, someone reminded me to beware since it is the day before Thanksgiving. Last year before Thanksgiving, Richie Petitbon quietly put an announcement on the bulletin board saying that any Redskin player who wanted a free turkey simply had to go to the Giant Food store nearest his home, give his name to the manager, and pick up his turkey. That's exactly what we did and everyone got the same result — a lot of strange looks and no free turkey. However, it seems Richie's prank paid off. One of the higher-ups at Giant found out about the hoax and was mad that the company hadn't thought of it. So today we all received special certificates entitling us each to a free turkey for tomorrow's dinner.

The sun broke through while we were on the practice field, and it helped turn a sluggish practice into a sharp one. We ran 12 "good ol' striders" *after* practice! Those sprints genuinely wear me out, but I still forced myself to do some light weight lifting to keep my strength up.

Larry Brown and Jerry Smith received MVP awards against Atlanta, and Paul Laaveg got the Gator Award for his record-breaking week of bitching.

Thursday, Nov. 23, Thanksgiving Day

Practice started early today so we could get home to those Thanksgiving dinners and to the Dallas-San Francisco game on television. Practice was short, but we looked good. We're still not getting credit around the country. Various writers are saying we'll fold in the stretch. A victory Sunday will assure us of a playoff spot; maybe we'll get some credit then.

My wife's sister, brother and nephew came in from Ohio for Thanksgiving. We also had my "little brother," Nolan Cowens, and two little friends of mine from Junior Village. I just couldn't see letting them spend Thanksgiving Day around Junior Village watching television by themselves.

Thanksgiving was a great day in all respects. The dinner was fantastic, and the Cowboys–Forty-Niners game made the day complete. San Francisco blew the Cowboys off the field, completely dominating the game and winning 31-10. That puts us two full games ahead of Dallas, and I know there are a lot of thankful Redskins today.

After dinner and the game, I took Nolan home and dropped my two friends off at Junior Village. I always hate leaving them there. I sure wish I could afford it — I'd like to keep them myself.

Friday, Nov. 24

We had a very sharp workout today. Everyone was lifted by the Forty Niner win. Coach Allen reminded us, "That win is only good to us if *we* continue to win and continue to keep the pressure on the Cowboys." We all seem aware of that. Every week the dollar signs grow larger in everyone's eyeballs. It's going to be hard to keep us from that pot of gold.

Saturday, Nov. 25

Concentration is part of our routine now. It shows in our meetings and on the field. Stringbean, the official, had few penalties of any sort to report for the week. We reviewed our Green Bay films and, while everyone is still impressed with the Packers, we are also confident and prepared.

Sunday, Nov. 27

Green Bay was our toughest opponent to date. Our offense had trouble moving their big defensive team at first, and it seemed that we spent most of our time punting the ball. The Packers had a chance to score very early in the game when their outstanding rookie placekicker, Chester Marcol, tried a field goal from around the 38 yard line. Marcol makes Green Bay a scoring threat anytime they get past midfield. But our specialty teams came through again, blocking Marcol's attempt. Later in the quarter, however, we were not so fortunate, and Marcol booted a good one from 50 yards out, making it 3-0 as the first quarter ended.

In the second quarter, Pat Fischer ruined a Packer drive by intercepting a Scott Hunter pass and returning it to their 37. After a great 25 yard run by Charley Harraway and a couple of clutch passes, we were on Green Bay's two. Then Larry Brown, who had a good but very physical game, vaulted over a Packer defender for a touchdown. Larry smelled pay dirt, and although the defender had a clean shot at him, Larry just leaped over him and tumbled head-over-cleats into the end zone.

Later in the second quarter, our defense clamped down and forced a Packer punt. Billy came out and made quick work of Green Bay. He took our offense 70 yards in six plays, firing some beautiful passes to Roy Jefferson and finally hitting Jerry in the end zone from 25 yards out. It was Jerry's seventh touchdown of the season. That made the score 14-3 and things were looking up with 2:00 left in the half. But we faltered on defense and Marcol hit a 37 yarder just before the half ended, cutting our lead to 14-6.

The third quarter was a bruising defensive battle which in essence determined the outcome of the game. No points were scored, but we appeared tougher as the game wore on. There were no signs of anyone on our side being over the hill. Much of the quarter was spent chasing and nailing rookie Jerry Tagge, who had replaced Scott Hunter at quarterback after Fischer's second quarter interception. Tagge has a strong arm, but our coverage, pass rush, and five man line were a little too much for a rookie to figure out. We gained control of their running game, so Tagge was in a very unenviable position in his second appearance as a pro.

Early in the fourth quarter, Tagge showed his poise by firing a 15 yard strike to Dave Davis for a first down on our six. MacArthur Lane ran over for a touchdown making the score 14-13 with about 12 minutes left to play.

Billy took over on our 22, and he calmly marched us to a touchdown, eating up six minutes in the process. Billy really thinks things out there; his play calling gets better and better. He mixed five passes (three to Charley Taylor and two to Roy,) with short runs by Larry, and successfully wore Green Bay down. Billy ended the drive with a five yard toss to Charley Taylor, and we were ahead to stay, 21-13.

Verlon and Bill Brundige pressured Tagge for the rest of the game, although Marcol did kick his third field goal of the day with 2:30 left. But we didn't give the Pack another chance to see the ball, and with a minute or so left those hungry Redskin fans began singing, "Amen." They have waited a long time. The game ended 21-16.

It was a great day. We clinched a playoff spot, held Brockington to 42 yards and Lane to 71, and we passed successfully against one of football's most stubborn pass defenses. To top it off, I was given a game ball. It's incredible how absolutely melodious the "horse's ass" song can sound when you're clutching a game ball.

The Atlanta contest is halted to present game ball to Larry for surpassing the thousand yard mark.

Loose ball in Green Bay game pursued by me, Verlon (89), and Mike Bass (41).

Billy barks signals against The Pack.

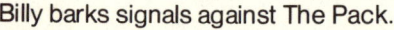

The Philadelphia Eagles (3)

Monday, Nov. 27

Bonnie Westley, the head of my fan club, who operates out of the same building our mobile homes offices are in, decided she would like to own the Redskins. "What would you do if you did own the team?" I asked her.
"I'd move it to Colorado," she said assuredly.
"Colorado? Why Colorado?" I asked, a little surprised.
"Because I just love to snow ski," she replied.
"Well, if your team enjoys skiing too," I said, "you're going to have an awful lot of busted up ball players and you won't win any games."
She mulled that over for a moment, and then she said, "Well, I would still have a lot of fun skiing."
Edward Bennett Williams, watch out!

Tuesday, Nov. 28

We need a victory over the Eagles in Philadelphia this Sunday to clinch the division title — Coach Allen reminded us of that today immediately after congratulating us on our

Green Bay win. I know he's concerned about having us mentally prepared for Philadelphia, since we beat them in the pre-season and in our fourth regular season game. Adding to the problem of having us ready is the fact that the Eagles were humiliated 62-10 by the Giants this past Sunday. They will be an angry bunch with something to prove against us.

In critiquing our films of the Green Bay game, we realized how fortunate we were that a couple of their deep passes weren't caught. We'll have to keep Philadelphia's fine deep threats, Harold Jackson and Ben Hawkins, from getting deep on us this Sunday.

Most Valuable Player awards for the Green Bay game went to Charley Harraway and Roy Jefferson. Wilbur's wine award went to Billy Kilmer again. He must be starting his own collection by now.

We had a good workout today without pads. We're a pretty loose bunch right now, and I guess that's to be expected after our two big wins. With the Eagles coming up, I just hope we're not too loose; we can't let the Giants' score fool us.

Wednesday, Nov. 29

The Eagles' receivers, Hawkins and Jackson, have been having a good season even though teams are primed for passes against Philadelphia because the Eagles have had trouble getting any ground game going. Coach Allen pointed out today that Philadelphia's defense, especially the front four, is not as bad as its showing against the Giants would indicate. In fact, the Eagles haven't been completely out of many games this year. They've moved the ball well between the twenties, but they can't seem to get the points on the board.

Larry Brown has been a workhorse all year, and his load

is starting to take its toll. The Eagles are always hard on Larry and Sunday could be rough on his already bruised body. We're all concerned about it.

Thursday, Nov. 30

Our practice was a little sluggish today. Having beaten the Eagles twice already (once in exhibition), we seem a little too confident. But two things will keep us from being flat — (1) Philadelphia always plays a hard-hitting game against us, and (2) we can clinch our division with a win. We'll come through.

Duke Zeibert brought us another huge victory cake today. While we were stuffing ourselves I was teasing Duke. I guess I was calling, "Hey, Duke," quite a bit because Talby picked it up and started calling out, "Hey, Duke," to me. Pretty soon several other guys picked it up. It seems to have caught on a little, because guys kept it up most of the day. "Duke" Owens? Somehow, it doesn't quite sound right.

One "Duke" who influenced my career was J.D. "Duke" Smith, the former Dallas running back, a veteran of several years when I first came up with the Cowboys. Dallas had drafted an outstanding crop of rookies in 1965, among them Bob Hayes, Jethro Pugh, Mitch Johnson, Ralph Neeley, and Craig Morton. We were a cocky bunch and we could get a little rowdy at times. J.D. would share a little of his personal philosophy with some of us when he felt we might be neglecting the team or ourselves. Above all else, I remember him telling me, "The most important thing you have to offer this game is your body. If you don't take care of it, no one else will."

J.D. is a great person. I guess there could be worse nicknames than Duke.

Friday, Dec. 1

Practice picked up a little today. As game time approaches, our concentration increases.

We've been getting some extra work on our specialty teams this week to insure a good performance from our kickoff and punt coverage teams against the Eagles. Philadelphia has moved the ball offensively against most clubs, but they have trouble putting points on the board. Their sustained drives have a tendency to falter when they get close to pay dirt. We want to prevent them from gaining good field position after a kickoff or punt; if we can force the Eagles to continually face long drives, our chances of being upset will be greatly decreased.

We're a little surprised that Philly is sticking with their rookie quarterback, John Reaves, when they have a more seasoned quarterback, Pete Liske, on the bench. With quick veteran receivers like Hawkins and Jackson, it would seem a veteran quarterback would be in order. However, the Eagles don't see it that way, and it's their choice.

I know Gary Ballman, the Eagles' tight end, well on the field. He's been around the league quite a while and he knows a lot of tricks. He's a big, bullish tight end, and although he isn't thrown to often, he has a habit of surprising a defender with a big catch. I don't think Reaves knows the value of throwing to a tight end, but I'm sure he'll realize it eventually.

Saturday, Dec. 2

After a light morning workout, we bussed to Dulles Airport and flew into Philly. The people in Philadelphia have a reputation for hostility toward their own teams. The Eagles' poor showing this year, particularly against the Giants last week, has the city screaming for blood. Ed Khayat, Eagles' head coach, appears doomed, and there's even talk that a group of fans are initiating legal action against the team for misrepresentation of product. That's a bad situation.

Sunday, Dec. 3

No wonder the Eagles have problems. I heard today before the game that no less than twelve Eagles have had major surgery and are out for the year. But that didn't stop them from giving us fits.

On their second play from scrimmage, the Eagles brought the boo-birds out with a fumble on their own seven. People were probably figuring we would pick up where the Giants left off. However, we moved the ball only as far as the two and couldn't get a touchdown out of it. We had to settle for a short Curt Knight field goal and a 3-0 lead. It was the Eagles' defense telling us that there would be no more 62-point nonsense.

The Eagles got a good drive going in the first quarter after holding our offense. On a pass play covering about 40 yards from Reaves to Ben Hawkins, they were on our 25 and driving. A few plays later we thought we had held them to a field goal, but a roughing-the-kicker penalty gave them a first down at our 10. At that point, Reaves hit six foot, eight inch receiver Harold Carmichael with a touchdown pass, and we were down 7-3 at the end of the quarter. We looked bad, so bad that our offense was unable to get a first down in the entire first quarter.

In the second quarter, our defense steadied, and good runs by Charley Harraway, coupled with a Kilmer bomb to Charley Taylor, put us at the Eagle two. We had faltered there early in the game, but Harraway wasn't about to let it happen again. He bulled over for a touchdown, making it 10-7 at the half.

We caught hell from Coach Allen at halftime. He pointed out our penalties and lax attitude as main reasons for our poor showing, mistakes we can't afford with the division title on the line. I think he hit home, although we didn't exactly blow the Eagles out of the stadium the second half either.

We picked up a field goal in the third quarter to make it 13-7. It was set up by a 35-yard pass from Billy to Larry. Larry twisted his already sore ankle early in the game, but he kept pushing himself. Then one chicken-shit Eagle kicked Larry in a pile-up and Larry had to hobble off the field. No one likes a ballplayer who pulls something like that. If you have to go after a man, do it face-to-face, not in a crowd where he can't defend himself. Even the Eagles were upset with their own man for that stunt. Fortunately, not too many ball players are that cowardly. Bob Brunet replaced Larry, who was hurt and nearly exhausted, for several plays, but Larry was playing again in the fourth quarter. No one can hold that man down.

Early in the fourth quarter, Curt kicked his third field goal of the game, making it 16-7 and indicating that he is out of his slump. The quarter was marked by an outstanding performance by Charley Harraway, who set up a touchdown with his running. The game ended at 23-7. We clinched the division title with a less than brilliant performance. Only Charley Harraway was truly outstanding today. As Billy told reporters after the game, "Charley Harraway is one man who really came to play football today." Charley received a game ball, and balls were also awarded to publicity director Joe Blair and trainer Joe Kuczo.

We were a happy group in the locker room and on the plane ride home, having secured step one in our drive to be

World Champs. However, we all realize that there are still two important steps to go — the NFC playoffs for the championship, and then a victory in the Super Bowl. We have a hard road ahead, but we are determined to win it all.

No one can catch like my roomo.

Charley Harraway's running kept us in the game at Philly.

Trainer Joe Kuczo receives a much deserved game ball, his first, after our victory over the Eagles, as Len Hauss and I offer congrats.

The Dallas Cowboys (2)

Monday, Dec. 4

We had a team meeting today, a rarity for a Monday. Coach Allen feels we need the preparation since we face Dallas this Saturday evening. It will be a great feeling going into Dallas as division champions; they're behind us for a change. For the Cowboys, Saturday is a must game; they need a victory to clinch a playoff spot.

Although understandably enthusiastic today after our Eagles win George Allen is somewhat cautious, pointing out that we've still got a long way to go. He's faced with some hard decisions; for example, how much rest should be given certain players, particularly Larry Brown who has been battered around so much this season. If he plays Larry and some of the other key men like Jack Pardee, there's the risk of injury which we can't afford right now. On the other hand, if he rests too many players, we may lose momentum going into the playoffs.

Coach Allen obviously fears a letdown since we have our division title clinched. There's no problem getting me psyched for Dallas. I always want to beat them, anywhere, any time. Although our plan for this game is no different than the plan we used to defeat the Cowboys in October, Coach Allen reviewed it thoroughly for us. We'll keep our defenses basic, letting the Cowboys do all the shifting. Coach Allen expressed specific concern that Dallas may use the halfback option pass with Calvin Hill throwing the ball to loosen our defense against the wide runs. The Cowboys used that play very effectively when Dan Reeves was playing with them, so Coach Allen wants us to be on the lookout for it. He also feels we'll be seeing more of Bob Hayes, since he's a veteran familiar with pressure games.

As one final incentive, Coach Allen unveiled a huge picture of the Super Bowl ring at our team meeting today. He told us that when we win our rings, he's going to put the largest diamonds on earth on them. That brought a lot of wild cheers from us. There are a lot of hungry ballplayers with something to prove on this team. We all liked the looks of that ring.

Tuesday, Dec. 5

I got to practice a little early today and found Speedy Duncan in the dressing room getting some treatment on his knee. Speedy has been replaced on the regular squad by Alvin Haymond, but he's not giving up. His spirits seem good, and he's always talking to other guys telling them to keep working. "You guys keep playin' hard," he was saying today, "and don't get hurt. You've got to win us some money."

Sportswriters report that Craig Morton has guaranteed a Dallas victory Saturday, and some other Cowboys are saying how they're going to beat us and go on to the Super Bowl. The Cowboys sure can talk; they seem loaded with that Dallas attitude that says, "Nothing's better than Texas." Well, they better realize that Washington's pretty damn good, too, especially in the area of football.

Those comments are especially surprising coming from Morton, who has never won any really big games for Dallas. We're going to throw our regular defensive strategy at Morton, and it should be enough to confuse him again. We'll disguise our defenses so well he won't know if we're going man-to-man, or zone, or blitzing, and all the while his offense will be jumping into its different formations. We'll see how smart Morton is then.

Coach Allen feels we overlooked big Ron Sellers in our first game against Dallas. Sellers is six-four, 225, and he has a habit of getting into the open in key situations. Morton looks for him in trouble spots. Sellers has great concentration and will find an opening if it exists. We can't give him one.

As far as the Cowboy runners go, Calvin Hill gets a lot of headlines with his great running ability inside and outside, but he's not as hard-nosed as his running mate, Walt Garrison. Coach Allen feels if we're physical enough, we can put Calvin out of the game, just as we did in Washington. But Garrison is extremely resilient and difficult to hold down.

Today's practice was only fair. Coach Allen is concerned about us getting our rest this short week. He's worried about a mental letdown more than a physical one. I'm sure he's wondering if we're willing to do some homework for this game, since we have our title wrapped up. A player must put forth effort on his own time. Lack of extra preparation could cost a game or two. Even though we have won our division, we can't afford any lazy habits at this point. They have a tendency to carry over.

Charley Harraway has picked up some bad habits from Dirty Biggs at lunchtime. Instead of looking for an entire lunch, Charley looks for snacks, like potato chips, to go with his sandwiches. He seems like such a nice fella, too.

Larry didn't work out at all today. He's having knee

problems. He also picked up several bruises in the Eagles game, one from the kick he received. Herb Mul-key looks good in his place, and he'll have a good test against Dallas. He'll also be running back kicks in place of Alvin Haymond, who injured his groin against Philly. The hungry free agent with no college experience will get his chance.

Wednesday, Dec. 6

It was a miserable, cold, rainy day today. Billy, Larry, Verlon, and Alvin Haymond all sat out practice.

Coach Allen was disturbed by the rain — worried about not getting in a good practice today — and he kept looking out the window during our morning defensive generals meeting. He reminded us that we must disguise our defenses to confuse Morton on Saturday. Mike Bass, Rosey Taylor, Pat Fischer and I will be lining up straight across, four to nine yards deep on every play. From that basic alignment, we can go into any defense we want but give the quarterback the same look every play.

We continued looking at Dallas films today. We will have seen eight or nine by the time the week is over, including some exhibition games. Each ballplayer updates his individual notes to study for the game. The preparation for each game seems unending.

I must confess: today I was guilty of scrounging some extra lunch. I didn't eat enough breakfast this morning, so I was looking for some hot soup to fill the void. At least I wound up getting mine honestly, borrowing a packet from Mike Bragg.

Everyone wore rain gear today, but it didn't keep us from slipping and dropping balls. It made a good practice nearly impossible, even on the astro-turf, which can get extremely slippery and hazardous at times. During practice someone quipped, "The rain will be ending shortly; Coach Allen has ordered it to stop." By sheer coincidence, I'm sure, at that moment the rain slowed almost to a stop. But within minutes it was pouring again, assuring us that Coach Allen did not possess that particular power.

Tonight I had my last speaking engagement of the season, and I was glad to get it out of the way. I want no distractions from this point on — the games mean too much now and they demand my complete concentration. I intend to give them just that.

Thursday, Dec. 7

Reading some additional information about Craig Morton today, I couldn't help but feel a little sorry for him in his situation on the Cowboys. His wayward comments about us aside, he has done a fine job for them this year. He's kept them on our heels all season, yet he's still catching hell from Dallas fans. They're screaming for Roger Staubach despite Morton's accomplishments. Craig will be trying to prove something against us for those fickle fans on Saturday, and we'll be trying to make him flop in front of them. Football's a tough game in more than one respect.

Larry Brown was talking about being well enough to play against Dallas, but Coach Allen has said "no." Larry's legs need the rest with the playoff games approaching. Bob Brunet, who will be sharing running back chores with Herb Mul-key in place of Larry, has been getting a good deal of attention from sportswriters. Bob is a very fast runner who would probably be first team with another club, and some writers have been asking him if he'd like to play more. Bob said, "If I could pick a team I'd like to play on, it would be right here behind Larry Brown." There's nothing to be ashamed of about being behind an athlete like Larry. Bob also pointed out that his work on the specialty teams makes him feel like he's not being wasted. Bob has to keep himself ready, physically and mentally, at all times; no substitute player knows when he might be called on to replace the first team man. I'm familiar with that situation myself. Bob has the kind of attitude typifying this year's Redskin team.

We were still missing that certain smoothness in practice today. Everyone's hustling, but there's something essential missing. Maybe it's because we're a little complacent now. That could be danerous, and Coach Allen has expressed his displeasure at such an attitude. The rain and astro-turf workouts don't help things much. I hope we're not going to be caught flat on Saturday.

Friday, Dec. 8

We traveled to Dallas today after a brisk morning workout, one of our best of the week. Before we left, Coach Allen reviewed our mistakes for the week with us. He had a lot to point out, especially in the area of penalties. The high number of penalties indicates our concentration was off, and Coach Allen took the opportunity to caution us on how dangerous a concentration lapse could be at this point in the season.

After settling down in our hotel in Dallas, I telephoned my sister who lives nearby. She wanted me to come to dinner, but it was getting too late. I probably could have made it back to the hotel in time for our 8:00 p.m. meeting, but I didn't want to risk it. Coach Allen might have thought I wasn't taking the game seriously, and that can get costly. But I was equally worried I'd miss out on the homemade sweet potato pies my sister always makes for me, so I persuaded her to meet me at the hotel after the meeting. She didn't let me down; she was there with her sweet potato specials. They won't last long once the scavengers catch sight of them.

Saturday, Dec. 9

It was another long wait for today's late afternoon game, but eventually I was in the new Dallas Stadium warming up for the game. The stadium is a little overwhelming at first, so new and modern. It's tailor-made for the fan; the entire fan section is covered by a dome, but there is a hole in the dome over the field, so the players still have to play in rain, sleet, snow, or whatever else arises.

Our game can only be described as a nightmare. We were out there physically, but I don't know where we were mentally. Coach Allen's fears of a letdown turned out to be well founded.

Actually, we played two ballgames today; one in the first half, which Dallas won, and one in the second half, which we won. The Cowboys played the first half with abandon, while we were being pushed around. They scored three touchdowns by early in the second quarter, while we had nothing to show. Walt Garrison and Calvin Hill ran all over us, and Craig Morton, who had guaranteed Dallas fans a victory, was connecting on his passes and looking like a prophet. It wasn't until the middle of the second quarter that we put points on the board after Curt Knight's field goal. But Morton, who is not supposed to be a scrambler like his teammate Roger Staubach, ran in for a touchdown late in the period. We went in at halftime losing 28-3.

At halftime, Coach Allen pointed out the painfully obvious to us. "We're being out-hustled and out-muscled," he said, "and we're being embarrassed on national television." It hit home. The second half was something else again.

Herb Mul-key had shown flashes of brilliance in the first half, but was overshadowed by our poor team performance overall. But from the opening kickoff of the second half, which he ran back for some 35 yards, he picked up our offense and nearly turned the game around. Billy marched us in for a quick score with a pass to Charley Taylor, making it 28-10.

In the middle of the quarter, after a Toni Fritsch field goal gave Dallas three more points, Billy led us to a quick touchdown. He did it with some smart play calling and a great 30 yard run by Herbie off a short pass. Billy then threw to Roy Jefferson to close the score to 31-17.

On defense, in the fourth quarter we held Dallas again and Billy and Herbie came in and blasted the Cowboys again. Herb seemed to gain momentum as the game went on. He's so quick he can convert a small amount of daylight into a long gain. He gave Dallas a real scare, setting up another Kilmer to Taylor touchdown.

With seven minutes left it was 31-24 and we had Dallas worried. We stopped the Cowboy offense and out came Billy and the boys looking to tie things up. That new stadium, which had been echoing with the wild cheers of Dallas fans earlier, grew quiet and tense. Dallas has been blowing big leads all year, and their fans sensed danger. However, Charley Waters, Dallas' young cornerback, intercepted a pass that bounced off several hands. With the ball on our 30 and about five minutes left, Toni Fritsch kicked another field goal and the game ended 34-24. Two more minutes and I feel we would have won.

As it was, I was glad to get out of Dallas.

Sunday, Dec. 10

A day of rest and introspection for some sad Redskins. We could read about the Cowboys saying to the reporters, "Who's the real power in our division?" We'll settle that question once and for all in our next game in three weeks; that is, *if* the Cowboys manage to win their first playoff game.

I concentrate from the sidelines.

Herb Mul-key responds to first real test versus the Cowboys.

Defense trying to get it together in Dallas.

The Buffalo Bills

Monday, Dec. 11

Despite his disappointment over Saturday's game, Coach Allen maintained his composure. He even gave us the day off, except for meetings, and didn't harp on our loss to the Cowboys; he knows we realize our letdown. In typical fashion, Coach Allen wrote off the loss as history and began preparing us for the Buffalo Bills and O.J. Simpson this Sunday at RFK. It will be our final regular season game.

Coach Allen pointed out that if we should lose to the Bills, and if Dallas should beat the Giants, our regular season records would be identical, 11-3. Although we would still be division champs, we all want to have the best record in our division to ourselves.

Jack Pardee was injured against Dallas as the result of being set up for cheap crackback blocks thrown by Dallas' wide receiver Lance Alworth. Alworth was the man in motion, but instead of going laterally until the ball was snapped, as stated in the rules, he would move toward the line of scrimmage. He'd catch Jack following the play and hit him from the blind side. Of course, blocking is part of the game, but deliberately setting a man up for a blind side block after a player gets an illegal running start has to be considered cheap. Coach Allen is understandably upset, and he's letting the Cowboys know how he feels about it. Jack probably won't be able to play against the Bills.

Tuesday, Dec. 12

The U.S. landed a man on the moon today. We can do so many great, complicated things in this country, but we so often fail at what should be the simplest of all acts—person-to-person communication. It disturbs and amazes me.

At our meetings today Coach Allen went over the Bills personnel. They're only about four players away from being a contender, with excellent offensive talent in quarterback Dennis Shaw, running back O.J. Simpson, and wide receiver J.D. Hill. On defense, they have big Walt Patulski, a rookie defensive end out of Notre Dame. However, most of the Bills are young, and their inexperience will be a plus for us.

We feel we can confuse Shaw with our coverage. He's primarily a short passer which means we can play the receivers a little tighter than usual without too much worry about them turning up field on us. Of course, we can't get too cocky or we'll get burned. We're confident we can out-execute the Bills. We will definitely have to control O.J., who needs around 100 yards to overtake Larry for the NFL rushing title. Simpson is a deceptive runner. His size is by no means awesome, yet he can run inside with the best of the power runners. Going outside, he just needs a flash of daylight and he's gone. What's more amazing is that Simpson doesn't have a very experienced line blocking for him. He can make yardage strictly on his own. Of course, we feel he hasn't come up against a front four as effective as ours is against the run. We have no secret plans for stopping him. We never key on any individual player, so we'll play standard defense against him and shut him off that way. If we can contain Simpson, we should beat Buffalo.

Wednesday, Dec. 13

Practice was a little flat today. We're having trouble focusing on Buffalo with the playoff game against Green Bay staring us in the face. I know we have to take each game one at a time, but sometimes it's hard to do.

Thursday, Dec. 14

Someone found out today that the Bills hold their practices on a parking lot because there has been so much snow in Buffalo. Compared to plush Redskins Park, the Bills' facilities may make them look like poor boys from the wrong side of the track, but they're still professionals. They have the ability to knock us off if we're not ready, regardless of who has better facilities.

The Bills have a lot at stake in this game. Some of those guys may fear their jobs are on the line, and they'll be trying extra hard for a good performance to impress the coaches. No team likes to be considered out of a game before it's even played, and the Bills are being called the underdogs in this one.

It was odd not having a victory cake to eat after practice today. Everyone missed it; it has come to mean more than just something good to eat.

Friday, Dec. 15

Now that we're nearing that playoff gold, I'm getting an

increasing number of phone calls at night. I'd like to know how my number gets around to so many people; it's not listed in the phone book and it's not available through the information operator. Yet, as the season goes on, more and more people I've never met or heard of call with good wishes, business deals, or mere idle conversation. Most people mean well, but they don't seem to realize that even an athlete enjoys some quiet time with his family. It's amazing how often a fan will call just to discuss a particular game, or give some advice.

The business offers are a different story. All too often, I'll get a call from someone who is going to make me rich. It usually involves something like me putting up most of the money, while he runs the business. Somehow, these deals sound a little fishy. I've come to believe many of these people feel that football players are non-thinkers who will jump at anything sounding like quick money. The weirdest offering I've had recently was from someone who wanted me to invest in developing orange groves in Florida. Considering the length of time it would have taken for the groves to produce, there's no way I would live to see oranges on the trees — or a return on my investment.

Tonight I just took the phone off the hook and forgot about it. Peace and quiet — it was great. I spent some of the time concentrating on my Buffalo assignments. Our practice today still left something to be desired.

Saturday, Dec. 16

I picked up my brother Ted at Dulles Airport this evening before going to the hotel. He's in from California for a little vacation and the cold weather kind of shocked him. After Ted, Patti, and I ate dinner out, they went home and I went to our team meeting. Coach Allen reviewed our basic plan: stop Simpson and force Shaw to throw long. Some psyching factors were reiterated: Larry's rushing title is at stake; we don't want our record tied with Dallas; we need momentum going into the playoffs.

We also learned that several regulars will see little or no action due to minor injuries: Larry, Jack Pardee, Mike Bass, Bill Brundige, Verlon, and my roommate Jerry. On offense, we'll be depending a lot on Herb Mul-key to pick up the slack in Larry's absence.

Sunday, Dec. 17.

It was a very long, very cold day for us today. So cold, in fact, we sharpened our cleats with a knife and a chisel before the game to get better traction on the frozen turf. But the Bills must have sharpened theirs better. Against a young Buffalo team that had only three wins for the year, we had one of our most frustrating games. Not only did we lose, 24-17, but our defense, so proud for its showing against the rush, gave up over 100 yards to O.J. Simpson, allowing him to outgain Larry Brown for the NFL rushing title. Of course, Larry hasn't played for the last two games so O.J. has a two game advantage on him, but that's not what the record books will show. We simply played terrible football.

We spotted the Bills a 10-0 lead in the first quarter on a field goal and a 48-yard touchdown run by Alvin Wyatt on an intercepted pass. Our offense controlled the ball for 10 of the first 15 minutes, yet we couldn't score and we were down by 10. We've come back from that kind of deficit before, but we were making a lot of mistakes and things looked bleak. However, another great performance by Herb Mul-key almost saved us.

Herb picked up an interference call on a 30-yard pass

from Billy which would have been a touchdown if Herb hadn't been interfered with. Instead, it was our ball on the Buffalo eight. Billy gave Herb the call and he followed some great blocking by John Wilbur for a touchdown, making it 10-7 in the middle of the second quarter.

We came out on defense and the Bills started to run over us. Simpson got rolling and Shaw mixed up his passes with some scrambles. With about two minutes to go in the half, Buffalo had pushed us to our own 10 and they were threatening to score. Shaw fired a pass which I almost picked off, but succeeded in knocking down instead. On the next play, he tried to pick on Pat Fischer, but Pat intercepted the ball in the end zone, saving us from real trouble before the half ended.

The Bills had the halftime edge in statistics in almost every offensive and defensive category. We were having great trouble getting settled, but in the third quarter it looked as though we finally had tamed Buffalo. Good runs by Herbie and a smooth, long-gaining end-around by Charley Taylor helped move us deep into Buffalo territory. Bob Brunet, who was spelling Harraway, plunged over for a touchdown to give us the lead at last, 14-10.

After the kickoff we came out and dug those extra-sharp cleats into the RFK turf and tightened up on the Bills. We forced them to pass and I came up with an interception on the sidelines. Someone pointed out later that the interception was my first of the year, a fact I hadn't realized. It doesn't matter to me how many interceptions I get in a year. There were some years when I was leading the team in interceptions, but we were still losing ballgames, and then they didn't matter. Just like today. I picked off the pass, and we drove for a field goal to boost our lead to 17-10, but we wound up blowing the game. We lost; that's all that matters. Despite our lead late in the game, we couldn't hold Buffalo's offense. O.J. ripped off some great runs and scored on a 21-yard sweep to tie the game at 17-17.

We finally lost on a pass that Herb Mul-key bobbled for an instant with two minutes left. The ball seemed to pop into the air and just before Herb grabbed it, a Buffalo defender whizzed by and intercepted it. He returned it about 45 yards to our three. From there, the Bills put the winning points on the board. It was a sour note on which to end the game and the regular season.

We were somber in the locker room, yet I think we were relieved to get back into some meaningful games. Looking around, I could see a team full of men who have something to prove. I'm sure after this game, our second loss in a row, we will be hearing the "over the hill" remarks again.

Over the hill, hell. This team is going to L.A.!

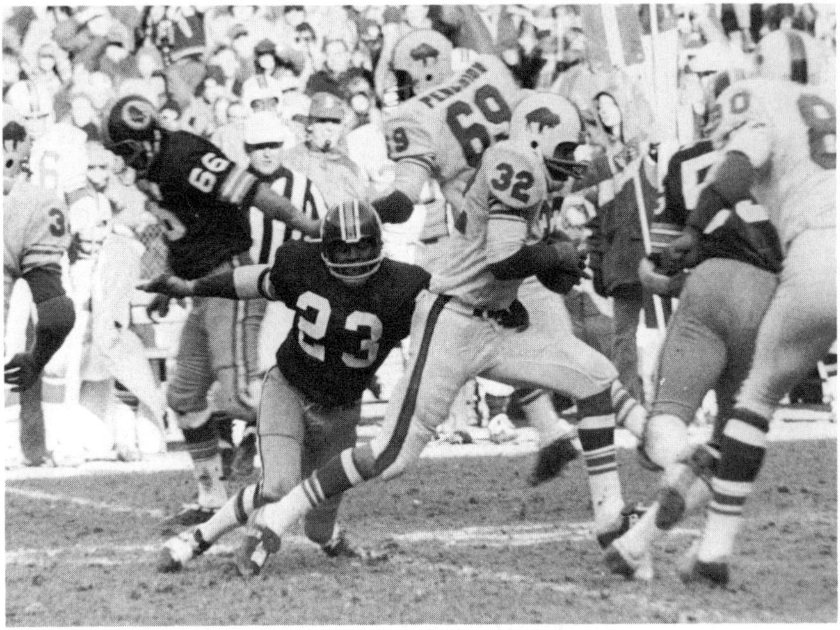

Come back to me, O.J.!

Brown and Harraway—a great combination.

Post-Season

The Green Bay Packers (2)

Monday, Dec. 18

We had the day off today after yesterday's humiliating defeat; the Bills didn't belong on the same field with us. I didn't especially want today off. I'm anxious to start preparing for Green Bay. They were very tough three weeks ago, and now, with a shot at the Super Bowl on the line, they're going to be ready for us.

A restaurant owner in Washington has been after the team to come to his place for a victory celebration since we won the division title. He invited us for dinner tonight, but I didn't go. It was a very nice gesture on his part, but it was just poor timing. We have the hardest part of the season still in front of us, and most of us feel that there's really nothing to celebrate until we win the Super Bowl. So I just decided to spend a quiet evening with my brother, daughters, and wife.

I left a little time for reviewing my Green Bay notes from our last game. This way I'll be able to spot anything different they might be doing as early as tomorrow morning when we begin to review the latest Green Bay films. That's what these games are all about — preparation and concentration. One missed play and all that green money disappears.

Tuesday, Dec. 19

Not too many guys went to the dinner party last night. It's good to know that most of us realize what kind of opportunity we have. Being able to go to the Super Bowl involves so many things — a sound, well prepared team, luck as far as injuries go, a smooth organization, etc. — that it could well be a once-in-a-lifetime opportunity. This year, with the team we've got, we should win it — but we have to be willing to sacrifice and lead what Coach Lombardi liked to call the "Spartan" life. It looks like most of us realize that.

Before our regular meetings started, I went upstairs and reviewed some Green Bay films on my own. I watched the Packer tight ends over and over, looking for any possible tipoff. I checked out how they line up, the number of steps they take on pass patterns, and what foot they pivot off. Packer tight ends are thrown to very infrequently; they are used more as interior linemen, as valuable assets to the great Green Bay running attack. The extra film study today didn't yield anything of great significance but at least I feel more familiar with their sets and tendencies.

Our practice was smooth and lively. We are an efficient bunch, and everything is falling into place. Our attitude is different than it was this time last year; we were then happy to achieve a playoff spot. Of course, we wanted to win the Super Bowl, too, but a playoff berth was satisfying at the time. This year, our goal has been from the start to win the Super Bowl, and the playoffs are just one important step on the way.

For Coach Allen, playoffs are nothing new. He took the Rams there twice, and last year, he took us. However, Allen has never *won* a playoff game. Well, this year it seems he's working harder than ever to erase that rap against him. He increased the pressure on us during practice today; he is continually studying films of the Packers. But what may be most important in Coach Allen's formula is that he analyzes *us* as thoroughly as he does our opposition. So he detects the other club's weaknesses, and then he analyzes what we can do as individuals to exploit them. Of course, all coaches follow this procedure, but few, if any, other coaches are as thorough as Coach Allen.

Wednesday, Dec. 20

At our meetings today, Coach Allen reviewed key points for the Packer game. He seemed even more confident than usual that he had Green Bay figured out. He did say that Green Bay is a bigger team than he originally thought, and he also noted that their offense is very similar to ours. He called for more gang tackling to bring down Brockington and Lane. Rosey Taylor and I looked at each other as if to say, "amen" to that because if those big guys should get up full heads of steam, we stand to be the last men to stop them. Each of us gives way about 40 pounds to those two.

We all watched films of Green Bay in their recent victory over the Minnesota Vikings. They dug in against the more experienced Vikings and gave them a rigorous, head-knocking beating. Fran Tarkenton was constantly trying to scramble away from the Packer defense. We were all very impressed, and, although we are confident, no one will be taking the Packers lightly.

Larry looked great in practice today. He's back at full speed for the first time since being injured by the Eagles. Charley Taylor and Roy were catching everything in sight and running their patterns perfectly. Jerry, however, is still nursing a hip pointer, so he wasn't at full speed today.

Jack Pardee worked all out today for the first time since being victimized by Lance Alworth's crackback block in the Dallas game. We all gave him a bad time, and I thanked him for finally getting around to practicing again. Gabby's response was cocky: "Well, I figured that since the money is on the line this time, I'd help you guys out and play Sunday."

All kidding aside, we were happy to see Gabby back. He calls our defensive plays, and today he was calling everything perfectly. Coach Allen often says that Pardee studies more than most quarterbacks in football. It shows.

Strange Wilbur suffered a badly bruised kidney against the Bills, and it's giving him trouble. Ray Schoenke, a seven year veteran, will take his place. Ray has been waiting to play this year and he's been keeping himself mentally and physically prepared, conferring with Strange about blocking assignments and swapping notes on Green Bay players.

Wilbur is eager to play, but since his condition is highly doubtful, he's willingly helping the man who will be taking his place. Just another example of the unselfish attitude on this team.

After practice I allowed myself one small diversion. Robin was in a Christmas play at church. After seeing those four and five year olds perform, I can see where Bill Cosby gets his great material on kids. One little girl came out and spotted her grandmother in the audience. She calmly said, "Hello, grandma," and then went on singing her part. A boy about five years old saw the microphone on stage, so he stepped up, grabbed hold of it, and started singing away, just like he has seen it done on television. Another girl stopped singing and came to the front of the stage so her mother could tie her shoe. I had to watch Robin out of the corner of my eye because if she had seen me looking right at her, she would have frozen for sure, as she was very nervous because I was watching. But she was great; they all were great.

Thursday, Dec. 21

My ribs have been bothering me lately, though I don't recall being hit there. I had them taped and worked on today before practice.

Coach Allen spent some time discussing Green Bay's linebacking trio of Dave Robinson, Fred Carr, and Jim Carter. He called them the "best linebacking unit in football." They are big, fast men who can plug holes quickly. Our linemen will have to fire out hard and fast to drive those three out of the play.

Coach Allen also stressed that because John Brockington had only 42 yards against us in our first encounter, he will be trying even harder to prove himself this time. Combined, Brockington and Lane gained more yardage than any pair of backs in the league, but we stopped them cold. This will provide added incentive for them and the rest of the Packers.

Green Bay feels they're a better team than the one we beat last month since they won pressure games against Detroit and Minnesota to make it to the playoffs. There have also been comments from the Green Bay area to the effect that we were lucky to win our first game against The Pack; that we were fortunate a couple of key passes were dropped. The way people throw the term "lucky" at us, you'd think we rode Lady Luck all the way this year. I think we must have at least a *little* talent.

Jerry was still at half-speed today, but he'll be a hundred percent by Sunday. He'd have to be hog-tied to be kept out of that game. Rooms is a very unusual tight end; he gives our offense an added dimension. Most tight ends are big and used primarily for their blocking ability. But Jerry not only blocks as well as any tight end around, he has a great pair of hands. He can beat teams long and short, and he's a great runner after making a catch. Inside the 20-yard line, I don't think there's a man in football who can cover Jerry one-on-one. In fact, other teams respect Jerry so much that they don't dare double-team our outside receivers and chance ignoring Jerry. He'll burn any team that tries it. True, Coach Allen likes his tight ends a little bigger, so Jerry and Mack Alston have been alternating lately. But one thing's certain about Jerry Smith — he may not be the biggest tight end around, but there's none better. He'll prove it every time he can.

Billy, Roy Jefferson, Charley Taylor, Chris Hanburger, and Larry all received word today that they made the NFC Pro Bowl team. They all deserve it, and I'm sure they were pleased. But I'd bet they'd all say it means nothing unless we win the Super Bowl.

Friday, Dec. 22

It was bitter cold today. I thought about the Packers practicing in the warmth of North Carolina, but I was only envious for an instant. After all, we're practicing in the kind of weather we'll be playing in, while the Packers will have that adjustment to make.

We were fired up and confident today. We've got our strategy down, and we're in good shape physically except for John Wilbur. All that's left is for us to go out and execute, and, of course, that's the crucial part. All the preparation and study will go right down the drain if we don't dictate to Green Bay and play sound football.

Wilbur had to sit out practice again because of the kidney injury he suffered against Buffalo. His chances for playing Sunday look pretty slim right now, but I know that if there's any way at all, Strange will be in that Green Bay game. Ray Schoenke is doing a great job in his place, another example of how important it is to be physically and mentally ready at all times. Ray stepped into John's place and took over with ease. That's another big advantage of having veterans backing up veterans.

Coach Allen's confidence is growing each day. He's been watching films again and he told us that he just doesn't see how Green Bay can adjust to the defenses we're going to throw at them. It's going to be a very tough situation for young Scott Hunter. We'll use the five-man line on and off, and if it stops his running game, he'll be forced to call audibles off at the line. Then he can't rely on Bart Starr. Hunter will be on his own on the field, and then he'll be ours.

As Coach Allen put it today, "There's no room for air at this point. The most miserable feeling a player or coach can have is to have to sit back and watch the playoffs or Super Bowl on television. There are all those teams that would like to be in our shoes, but it's our turn now. Let's take advantage of it. There's no room for air now." There's no one on this team who is thinking about coming up for air either; we're a bunch of hard-working Redskins.

Chester Marcol, the Green Bay placekicker, is one of Coach Allen's biggest concerns since he has such good range. We blocked a field goal against him in the first game, and the special teams are working on pressure strategy for the upcoming game. Coach Allen feels Marcol hasn't been put under intense pressure this year, except when he faced us. So every time he kicks we have to have some men bearing down on him. Coach Allen has also noticed that many of Marcol's kicks stay low for a longer time than most kickers' do. That makes him more vulnerable to a blocked kick, and Coach Allen feels we will be able to rattle the rookie Marcol decisively.

We had such a great practice today that Coach Allen was

as enthusiastic as a child at Christmas during our afternoon defensive meeting. So were we. We reviewed our entire game plan. Then we went over Green Bay's tendencies for every conceivable down and yardage situation. We discussed what defense we would be in, what our coverage would be, and what variations we might use.

Coach Allen was so pleased with everything today that he announced there would be no workout tomorrow. We'll have meetings, but that's all. That was greeted with a big cheer. I know this — I've never seen a group of ballplayers as high, ready, and eager as we are.

As I was dressing to leave, Pat Fischer was talking about Christmas presents and I realized that I hadn't bought my most important one yet. I had seen a ring for Patti that I liked, so when I left practice I stopped at a jewelry store and bought it for her. I owe Fischer a thank you for reminding me that Christmas is drawing near.

Saturday, Dec. 23

Curiosity seekers were at Redskins Park today almost as early as the players. All of these well-meaning Washington area fans wanted to check us out to make sure we've got our game together. Our aging but able one-man security force, Double-O Boynton, has been keeping busy chasing them away. Even though the weather has been freezing, Double-O still pedals around on his bicycle asking people to leave. He is really conscientious. Today he was pedaling around the practice field when he spotted something. Talby started ribbing him. "Point, Double-O, point," he yelled laughing. "Now, hold. Now go get him, Double-O." Sure enough, Double-O had spotted someone outside the fence and he went after him. Double-O rarely gets rattled.

Green Bay has a strong kick returner in Ken Ellis. Our special teams coach Marv Levy has been preparing us to stop him. We have to keep him from getting the sidelines on us.

At our team meeting, Coach Allen again showed the king-sized picture of the Super Bowl ring. This time he said that he would send Super-Sis out to find the biggest diamonds in the world for the ring. Big Sis could carry a whole lot of diamonds in those enormous arms of his. Sis is sort of Coach Allen's favorite, and he broke into a big grin and said, "That's right, Coach." Sis is going to play a big part against Green Bay tomorrow in the five man line and he is sky high for this game.

We reviewed what Coach Allen calls "in case" defenses at our defensive meeting. These are specially prepared defenses in case our basic plan doesn't work. This way our counterattack won't be subject to improvisation.

After our meetings we were free to go home until check-in time at the hotel. Tom and I got to my place in time to watch the Oakland-Pittsburgh playoff game. We sat and ate a great lunch while watching the Steelers and Raiders pummel each other. Pittsburgh dominated most of the game, but could put only seven points on the board. Then, in a last-ditch effort to save the game, Oakland quarterback Darryl Lamonica was replaced by young Ken Stabler. Stabler got a sustained drive going with some fine hustle and some gutsy play calling, and with a little more than one minute left to play, he scrambled 30 yards for a touchdown. The Raiders were a happy bunch, but not for long.

With a matter of seconds left, on the game's final play, Pittsburgh quarterback Terry Bradshaw wound up and threw a desperation pass intended for Frenchy Fuqua. The ball was deflected either by a defensive back or by Fuqua himself into the arms of the Steelers' prize rookie Franco Harris. Harris was already running at full speed, and he never broke stride on the way to the game winning touchdown. Harris made a heads-up play, the kind that wins ballgames involving evenly matched teams. On the other hand, Harris ran right past one Oakland defensive back who was holding his hands up in victory. That defensive man made the fatal mistake — he relaxed for a split second during the game. Tom Skinner had been saying throughout the game that the most alert team would win. He was right. Harris was alert, and he won the game, an all-time great cliffhanger, for the Steelers.

The Dallas-San Francisco game also had an exciting finish. It agitated me to watch the game because the Forty-Niners manhandled Dallas throughout the game, but suddenly got conservative in their play toward the end. They wound up handing Dallas a gift and the Cowboys accepted a 30-28 victory after trailing 21-3. Craig Morton had a rough afternoon and he was replaced late in the game by Roger Staubach. It was a test under fire for Staubach who is trying to come back from a separated shoulder. He brought the Cowboys back when Preston Riley of San Francisco fumbled an onsides kick and Dallas' Mel Renfro recovered. Dallas went on to score, and I felt like kicking the television set in. I was also sick of hearing about the so-called "great" Cowboy team. Commentators try to compare them to the Lombardi-coached teams of the sixties, but in my mind they don't even come close.

I turned to Tom Skinner and said, "When they come into Washington, the Cowboys won't get any breaks like that. We'll beat Green Bay and we'll beat Dallas too."

Tom just nodded agreement.

My teammates shared my disgust at the outcome of the Dallas game. Actually, we'd rather beat the Cowboys on our way to the Super Bowl than any other team. It's that Dallas attitude that bugs us.

After calming down, we reviewed our strategy, special team objectives, and still another Green Bay film. When it was over, I went upstairs and delved into my hot fudge sundae.

Sunday, Dec. 24

It was cold and rainy today — Redskin weather. I was up even before our 7:00 a.m. wake-up call, thinking about the job ahead of me. At 7:30 I went to vespers where Tom Skinner gave an inspirational talk on ambition, character, togetherness, and man's relationship with Christ. After vespers, we all went to our pregame meal, and for the first time in I don't know how long, I didn't feel like eating. I had a little meat and a few bites of toast, but that's all the butterflies would allow.

Charley Harraway, Tom and I rode to RFK with Chris Hanburger. Not one mention of Green Bay was made. We arrived about 9:40 a.m., and by that time the car was completely quiet. It was odd, but when we were walking toward the stadium we crossed paths with a couple of Packers, but no one spoke. The importance of this game was evident to us all.

Our locker room was intense prior to the game. It was a good, confident atmosphere conveyed by veterans who know what they must do. I looked around and said to myself, "This team knows where its head is."

We reviewed our plans and opposing personnel yet another time before taking the field. During early-birds, I saw my former defensive backfield coach, Don Doll, now a Packer coach, on their sidelines. I went over and talked for a minute or two. I told him, "Here we go again, Don. This is what it's all about." He just nodded. Significantly, neither of us wished the other luck. For as much as I like and respect Don — I think he's head coaching material — I just couldn't wish him luck in this game, nor could he wish it to me. I guess we're both honest.

Coach Allen, whose enthusiasm hasn't ebbed all week, said confidently before we took the field for the game, "I just know we will play one of our greatest games today." He was prophetic.

We went out and brawled with The Pack. The first quarter was marked by some of the hardest hitting I've ever been involved in. We were letting each other know what kind of day it would be. Neither team scored in that first quarter and we were given a scare when Billy was blasted hard on one play and had to be helped off the field. He was a little woozy, but he returned to the game the next time we had the ball. It's been said that when Billy was with New Orleans, the Saints gave all their players psychological tests on various topics, and that Billy's tests showed he has no sense of fear at all. He has guts; he proved it again today.

Though the outcome of the first quarter was the same — zero-to-zero — we felt we had an edge psychologically. It was evident the five man line was confusing Hunter and it was also evident that we were taking away their bread-and-butter — the run. Coach Allen would wait until Bart Starr sent in a play, and then he'd send in a defensive change. This put Hunter on his own, and our veteran defenses had the young man confused.

In the second quarter we spotted Green Bay a quick three points as the rookie, Chester Marcol, showed poise booting a 45 yard field goal. But the Packers were still having big problems moving the ball, and I wasn't worried.

Herb Mul-key took Marcol's kickoff two yards deep in the end zone and raced upfield for a 40 yard return. Speedy little Herbie almost broke it, but he was pulled down by the last man with a shot at him. Using the clock excellently, Billy moved the ball to the Packer 30 with about 3:30 left in the half. Then, after setting Green Bay up with our running game, he fired a touchdown pass between two defenders to Roy Jefferson. Roy never broke stride, and Curt's extra point gave us a 7-3 lead.

I guess Hunter and the rest of those young Packers figured we old Redskins were going to coast into halftime with a four point lead while they ran out the clock. They were wrong.

We shut off the Packer running game as soon as they took over the ball. When Hunter went to pass out of desperation, he was sacked around our 15 yard line. Ron Widby's punt was nearly blocked by half of our specialty team, and because of the pressure, Widby got off a poor kick. We took over at our 40 and, with 30 seconds left, Curt booted a field goal to give us a 10-3 lead at halftime. Curt's kick was about a 45 yarder. It seemed like an hour from the time it left his foot to the time it went through the uprights. It was an extremely high kick and the entire crowd seemed to get quiet, so quiet that I swear I could hear the ball when it nicked the back of the crossbar. After that, I just heard a lot of cheering, my own included.

As they walked off the field at halftime, the Packers seemed stunned. We had burned them on offense and defense in one quarter. Their running game was nonexistent, and Hunter was faced with an increasing amount of audibles. On the other hand, *our* confidence was surging even higher.

The third quarter was another one of those bone-crunching periods that we get into so often against The Pack. Neither offense had much luck and Mike Bragg's strong punting kept Green Bay against the wall. Finally, with about two minutes left in the period, Larry and Charley Harraway began breaking some gains following the determined efforts of our offensive line. We drove to the Packer 33 and then stalled, but

Curt was perfect on another field goal making it 13-3. At that point, the crowd sensed victory.

Hunter calmed the crowd in the fourth quarter after he hit four straight passes. He called some nice plays during that span, and I think everyone began wondering if some of that "last minute magic" that had marked the other two playoffs was going to strike again. Pat Fischer supplied the answer. After his successful string of pass completions, Hunter tried to get Brockington rolling on a sweep. Pat Fischer is about 60 pounds lighter than Brockington, but he met him head-on, one-on-one, and drove the big man to the ground single-handed for a five yard loss. The Packers wound up punting away, and they saw their hopes diminish greatly.

Billy marched the offense downfield from our own 15 to around the Green Bay 30, using Larry to cover 30 yards of the drive on five carries. It looked like we were headed for a touchdown, but we got overanxious and penalties forced us to call on Curt again. Curt, the man in a slump for a long time during the season, showed how tough he gets under pressure. He boomed his third field goal of the game, making it 16-3 with 2:30 left.

Green Bay was dead, and Scott Hunter, throwing in desperation, was intercepted by Chris Hanburger to seal the coffin. At that point we started our backslapping and congratulating. The other playoff games may have been won on last minute magic, but we don't give anything away.

The game's most outstanding individual performance was put in by big Manny Sistrunk. They just couldn't handle Super-Sis. He made one particular hit on MacArthur Lane that I'll never forget, and neither will Lane. Lane darted for a hole and I moved in and got set to bring him down. Before I could hit Lane, Sis appeared out of nowhere and hit him head-on. When he hit him, Sis let out a yell like, "Whaaaaa!"

Sis stood over him and Lane just sat there for a moment glassy-eyed and said, "Gaaawd Daaaamn!" After that hit, Manny scared a lot of people on the field, including his own teammates. A man just isn't supposed to be able to hit that hard.

    Manny and everyone else was making a lot of noise in our locker room. We celebrated with modest refreshments like ice cream and soft drinks, saving the more serious refreshers until after our Super Bowl win. We laughed and joked and responded to interviews. All the reporters were getting their questions in and I couldn't help thinking how far we've come since being dubbed "over-the-hill," and "lucky" all year. We earned our spot in these playoffs and we earned today's win. And I knew as I looked around that underneath Coach Allen's wide grin as he clutched his game ball, and behind the laughter of the team, we were already beginning to prepare ourselves for the Dallas Cowboys.

    Merry Christmas, Washington!

Pardee and the gang head-to-head against Green Bay.

Defense—Ron McDole (79), Jack Pardee (32), Diron Talbert (72), and Dirty Biggs (89)—stacks up MacArthur Lane.

The Dallas Cowboys (3)

Monday, Dec. 25

Christmas couldn't have been more merry. I was one happy Santa Claus, and everyone was pleased with the presents.

Tuesday, Dec. 26

This week begins the showdown we've all been waiting for against Dallas. But today was also a sad day for our country. Former President Harry S. Truman died today. Truman's most admirable quality was his ability to act when the situation was most difficult. Physically and mentally, he was a tough man.

Our locker room was a little more noisy than usual, reflecting our Green Bay victory and the growing anticipation of playing Dallas. Even though it was a rainy day, and we knew we would be working out on the astro-turf, our spirits were still sky high.

There was a lot of joking and laughing about Christmas scenes in homes of various players. Some had too much turkey, some had tales about kids tearing down trees. Walter Rock was being ribbed by Ron McDole a lot about the dinky tree he bought for his kids. It was so small his wife tried to get him to plant it in their back yard and buy another one.

McDole had one of his Christmas gifts with him, a dog leash with an imaginary dog on the end of it. The leash moves as if there is a real dog on it, and Ron has it perfected. One of his specialties is imitating cat and dog fights. He had the locker room in an uproar with the leash, and his barking and meowing.

We've been looking forward to this rematch for so many reasons. First of all, it's the rubber game for this year. Secondly, we felt that last year, had we gotten past San Francisco in the playoffs, we had the team to beat the Cowboys and go on to the Super Bowl; we never got the chance to prove it, but we will this year. In the third place, it's Dallas, and they always bring out the most competitive side in us. When we beat them this Sunday, no one should be saying anything about us sharing the title with them.

Everyone should be ready to play. Larry's nursing a slight hamstring pull. Terry Hermeling has a touch of flu, and Strange's kidney is still troublesome, but they have the week to recover. Knowing that we'll be playing Dallas is better medicine than any doctor could prescribe.

Awards for the Green Bay game went to Larry, Manny, and Gabby. Speedy's six pack went to Rusty Tillman, and John Wilbur gave his wine to Coach Allen.

Coach Allen could hardly wait to show us the Green Bay films. He said he was surprised the Packers didn't adjust better to the five man line since they had seen it before. I guess Green Bay just didn't think we would come back with it again. The films bore out the fact that Gabby called a defensive game as close to perfection as possible.

When the films were over, Coach Allen said, "We can't spend any more time looking at these films now. The Cowboys think they can get by us without any trouble. Boy, do they have a surprise coming."

Though the Cowboys are noncommittal on who their quarterback will be, Coach Allen feels certain they'll go with Roger Staubach. Staubach led the comeback against San Francisco, and he led them to last year's Super Bowl win. Regardless of who quarterbacks, we know what we have to do — keep our defenses basic no matter how much shifting Dallas does, hit the Cowboys for all they're worth. Dallas never does well against very physical teams.

I thought we had a good practice, but Coach Allen wasn't as pleased as I thought he'd be. He felt we were a little too loose and weren't concentrating as well as we should have. I think he was using a little psychology on us, making sure we don't get too cocky over our Packer win.

Chris Hanburger was griping (as usual) at our afternoon defensive meeting because a few guys straggled in after showering. The sooner we get everyone to the meeting, the quicker we can get started and get out at a reasonable hour. Chris kept grumbling away, but it didn't have much effect on the latecomers. It always amazes guys how a grouch like Chris can be meek as a lamb around his lovely wife and two little girls. But then, I know how women can affect us big, tough, grouchy men.

Wednesday, Dec. 27

Jack Pardee was at Redskins Park early today getting treatment on his knee when I arrived. It's the knee he injured in our last game against Dallas when Lance Alworth hit him with a crackback block. The papers today were reviving the

Alworth incident, building it up as a grudge against the Cowboys. Alworth was reportedly implying that if we didn't like it, we'd know where to find him Sunday. Alworth is quite a bit smaller than Gabby, so guys were ribbing the latter about what he's going to do about it. He just laughed and said, "We'll see how he comes down on me Sunday. I'll take it from there."

I don't feel Alworth is a dirty ballplayer or anything like that. He's supposed to be going laterally when he goes in motion from the flank, but since he goes upfield while in motion it should be illegal. However, no one has called it. What's probably going to happen is that with all the controversy over the play, the Cowboys will be afraid to use it. If Alworth does try it again on Gabby, I feel sorry for him.

Coach Allen told Gabby at our generals meeting to "knock Alworth's head off" if he tries the crackback again, not that Gabby had to be told. Coach Allen reviewed our basic strategy, which is to keep our defenses thoroughly disguised, but simple. He said we would use very few blitzes, and he also said he felt Bob Hayes would be playing.

At the defensive meeting, Coach Allen indicated that we must have a good performance from our front four, particularly against Staubach. He branded Alworth's talk as "typical" of the Cowboys, and he told us to forget it and just force Dallas to play our game. Then he showed films of the Dallas-San Francisco win which Dallas lucked into.

Practice was good today, and Coach Allen was more pleased today than yesterday. Hermeling was still slowed by the flu, and now Bob Burnet has joined him. But the rest of us were going strong. I can't imagine losing to the Cowboys.

Thursday, Dec. 28

I watched Dallas films on my own this morning at Redskins Park. I was having a little trouble concentrating because my body was feeling pretty run down. I checked in with trainer Joe Kuczo, and he immediately issued me a surgical mask. He thinks I've picked up the flu, as have several other players. In fact, there were so many surgical masks, the place looked like an operating room. It's an inopportune time for the bug to hit.

We reviewed various charts on Dallas today at our team meeting. The most interesting one, by breaking down their scoring into quarters, indicated that the Cowboys are very strong starters and then they fade. That means we have to lock them into our type of game early and hold them. If we can dictate early and get some points up, they'll have trouble getting untracked for the rest of the game.

There have been reports that Dallas' perennial All-Pro defensive end Bob Lilly will not play because of back trouble. Coach Allen's not believing a word of it. "Bob Lilly will play," said Coach Allen, "he's too great a competitor not to." That's it in a nut shell. Lilly won't miss a game like this.

Coach Allen was quite concerned about the flu victims, but he was more concerned about keeping it from spreading further. So at our various meetings, all flu cases had to sit together outside the meeting room and peer in through the doorways. That's where I sat as we reviewed more charts, films, and our just-in-case defenses. We very rarely need to use our just-in-cases, but we always keep up on them anyway. Coach Allen has been commenting frequently that the Cowboys "just don't check themselves out carefully," because he found several more important tendencies that show up in every film we watch. Of course, it takes Coach Allen's extra-careful inspection and study to discover and type them.

Practice was misery for me today. Every bone in my body was hurting. I was coughing, gagging, and choking the whole time. There was a slight breeze that chilled me to my aching marrow. I shouldn't have been out there, but I don't want to miss any thing. I found out after returning to the locker room that I had a temperature of 102. Trainer Kuczo suggested that I go straight home, go to bed, take aspirin, and drink plenty of juice. Instead, I went straight to a private meeting room and reviewed some more film.

I almost couldn't drive home, and when I finally arrived, I could barely drag myself out of the car. I never felt that bad in my life. Patti helped me into bed and took my temperature. It was up to 104, so she called our doctor and he told her to get me to the hospital for a shot. By the time we got there, my temperature was 105, and I thought I was fading fast. He gave me the shot and told me to go home and get to bed. He got no argument from me. I was thankful he didn't bury me.

Friday, Dec. 29

I felt like a new man when I awoke this morning. I don't believe I've ever had a more sound sleep. Although I was by no means one hundred percent recovered, the achiness was gone from my body and I was actually looking forward to practice.

Today's sports page headlines confirmed what we had suspected. Roger Staubach was named the starting quarterback for Dallas. Dallas Coach Tom Landry confirmed the report that he would bypass Craig Morton, Dallas' leader most of this year, for Staubach, a man who seems to be at his best in tough situations. It's quite a load on Staubach since he has missed so much playing time this year. He's got to be a little rusty, although he didn't look it against the Forty-Niners. But then, we're not the Forty-Niners.

Coach Allen is so confident that we'll be practicing next week for the Super Bowl, he had tarps delivered to cover the regular field so we won't have to practice on the astro-turf if the rain keeps up. Lately we've had to use the astro-turf frequently, and this late in the year that stuff is ten times more tiring on the legs than it is earlier in the season.

The trainer's room this morning looked like a hospital ward. There were at least ten additional guys with surgical masks on. Coach Allen is really concerned now, and he told us, "You guys can't get sick now." I think it's too late, Coach.

Coach Allen had separate meeting rooms set up for the sickly players again. Still, I've noticed that we are having very little trouble preparing for Dallas. After two games with them, we feel confident that we know what to do to win, and we'll do it.

After a long layoff, Dirty Biggs went on a tear today and I was his primary victim. He helped himself to some soup, but fortunately, I had some more stowed away so I didn't have to practice on an empty stomach as well as a run-down body.

Practice was not quite as good as Coach Allen or I had hoped. But with so many guys fighting the flu, it was understandable that some of the zip was missing. Two bright spots were Larry's running and Billy's passing. They both looked extremely sharp.

After practice Coach Allen announced that we would not work out tomorrow. He feels we are ready and that we need our rest instead of more practice time. I couldn't agree more heartily. I jumped on the scale today and realized this flu has knocked 11 pounds off me!

Saturday, Dec. 30

We reviewed and summarized all phases of our game plan today; offense, defense, and specialty teams. We reviewed Cowboy tendencies in each area. Nothing was left out. We know Dallas so well that if their field goal kicker,

Toni Fritsch, had one toenail longer than the others we would get an immediate updated analysis of the situation.

Bob Hayes called me today and asked me to visit him at his hotel. I told him I'd call him back if I could make it, but I didn't feel like seeing my opponent. I think Bob felt the same way, and was merely making a gesture as one old friend to another. We call on one another whether in Dallas or D.C., but this time I just couldn't get together with him with a game like tomorrow's coming up. It's a different sort of game this time.

At our defensive meeting this evening, we gave individual reports on aspects of the Cowboys' offense. We reported on things like how many times each quarterback looks off defenders, which way he looks first, how often he calls various running plays and what kind of releases the receivers have. These brief reports are often very helpful. Mo Pottios always has the funniest. No one thinks Mo is thorough in his preparation, but when he reports, he comes out with *everything*. Tonight he had some statistics on seemingly minor items, but they must have been correct because Coach Allen didn't challenge them, and he knows every statistic, so there's no way to bluff him.

Jerry and I ate our sundaes and then turned out lights off. We talked for a couple of hours about Dallas. Neither of us felt like sleeping, but not because we were worried; we were just anxious to get out and mop up the Cowboys.

Sunday, Dec. 31

I needed no wake-up call today. I was raring to go. Tom Skinner delivered his vespers talk and he was at his dynamic best. It might be hard for people to realize how important this man is to us, so to give people an idea of his message, I taped him this morning, and some of what he said follows:

"Someone said that a man without a mission is not really a man, because every person who is going to live life successfully has got to have some kind of purpose in life. There have been people who have made impressions on my life, that is, people I've read about in history, and one of these is a guy whose rap came about 30 years after Jesus. He was known as Paul. We had similar experiences; there were times in my life in which I wanted nothing to do with God or nothing to do with any mission or purpose. At the same time I considered myself an intellectual; I had all kinds of philosophical ideas as to why I didn't have to believe. But this guy Paul had some qualities about him that I think every man ought to have if he's going to live life successfully.

"One, he had a mission. Two, he had determination. Three, he didn't allow anything to stop him from reaching his goal. And four, he was a tremendously disciplined individual.

"Paul counted as garbage all the things that people live for, man. People live for prestige; people live for popularity; people live for fame and fortune; all those things that we are taught from childhood up are the things that really count. If a guy is going to be accepted in certain circles, they want to know where he comes from, what kind of family background he has.

"In the society in which we live, many times a man is judged by his wealth; he's judged by his family background; he's judged by his connections; and never by his character. Never by who he really is as a person.

"What Paul is saying is, 'Man, influence is great, prestige is great, money is a means to an end—that's great. But in the final analysis, if you compare it to what *really* counts, it's garbage'... Now, as I've said to you, that's either a sick mind or that's a man who's discovered something awful fantastic. I would almost have to dismiss that his mind was sick, because this guy Paul was too philosophical, too intellectual, too well read, too balanced a man in his demeanor to have been sick to that extent. Fanatic, maybe yes, but not sick. But then let's take a look at this guy Jesus. I mean, who in the world is Jesus Christ, that a guy would say, 'In comparison to what he stands for in my life, everything else is secondary.'"

Tom gave us about 25 minutes of thoughts like these to contemplate. Not once did he refer to football until he concluded with this prayer:

"There's a lot of discipline and sacrifice you have to make to play this game. You have decided that reaching your goal is worth what you have to pay to get there. And that's all Paul was saying, man. That's what it takes to be champions. You have to ask yourself if you're hungry enough for excellence, and those are also the standards for the kingdom of God. You've got to ask yourself, 'Is it worth it?'... It's a question of how a man committed to excellence is supposed to live... All I'm trying to do is to challenge others to a standard of excellence 24 hours a day in our total life style. And the basis of Paul's standard of excellence, the basis of my standard of excellence, is the person of Jesus Christ. Now, let's pray:

"Father, we thank you for the time that you're giving us together again. Lord, once again this afternoon the Redskin Community has to demonstrate its commitment to excellence. Father, you've been with us this whole season, and again we ask you to be with us today. Help us in our search for excellence; help us to *be* it. And help each one of us to individually discover the person of Jesus Christ and his ability to live his life out through us. We ask it in Jesus' name. Amen."

There wasn't a sound in the room while Tom spoke; there never is. He knows how to communicate. At our pregame meal after vespers, I felt the butterflies for the second week in a row and ate very little.

Since this was a 3:00 p.m. game, I arrived at RFK about one o'clock, courtesy of Chris Hanburger. Several players were already there. I was pleased to see no sign of surgical masks. We had beaten back the flu; now all that was left was Dallas. Looking around, it was hard to tell that many guys had been down with the flu at all during the week. Everyone was quiet, but ready to go.

This was the game that so many had waited so long for. The Redskins vs. the Cowboys, George Allen vs. Tom Landry, Bill Kilmer vs. Roger Staubach, and Lance Alworth vs. Jack Pardee.

The real 1972 NFC Champions rose up today and defeated the Cowboys, 26-3. We showed everyone what we knew all along.

From the outset it was evident that we would take control. The normally fast-starting Cowboys had difficulty moving out of their tracks in the first quarter. Neither team scored, but the first time we got our hands on the ball, Billy brought us from our own 20 to the Dallas 35. Undoubtedly, we would have put points on the board, but we lost possession of the ball on one of Larry Brown's infrequent fumbles. However, the Cowboys, with Staubach quarterbacking, had no chance against our defense. We stopped them cold everytime they had the ball that period. They didn't even come close to making a first down.

In the second quarter, we started to break away. Executing almost flawlessly on offense and defense, we drew first blood. With Billy doing some great play calling, we moved to the Dallas 11. The Cowboys held, but they couldn't stop Curt from kicking a field goal for a 3-0 lead. That got us moving.

The next time we had possession, Billy, whose throwing

arm has been criticized all year and most recently by Tom Landry, unleashed a 50-yard bomb into the hands of Charley Taylor. Charley had gotten behind young Cowboy cornerback Charley Waters and Dallas found us on their 21. After a couple of quick running plays, Billy sent Charley out on a slant pattern and he beat Waters for a 15-yard touchdown. Curt's extra point made it 10-0 with 5:00 left in the half.

The Cowboys came to life and scored on a Toni Fritsch field goal which hit the upright and fell over the cross bar. Preceding that field goal, Staubach scrambled for 29 yards, his only successful run of the day. Fritsch tried again just prior to the close of the half, but he was wide from 23 yards out. Ted Vactor applied some great pressure on that second kick, and he successfully caused Fritsch to miss. So our half-time lead stood at 10-3.

The third quarter was another stand-off with neither team scoring. When we came out to play after half-time it was raining and we knocked each other around in the mud. But again, we out-hit and out-hustled the Cowboys, and I think they were feeling a little added pressure at that point. Jerry, though he wasn't used as a receiver all day, played his usual aggressive, alert game and made one particularly crucial play in the third quarter. With the ball on our own 30, Billy had trouble handling the snap from Len Hauss and it squirted loose in our backfield. For a moment, it looked like no Redskin was even near the ball, and both Cornell Green and Lee Roy Jordan of Dallas had clean shots to pick it up and run into our end zone. But from nowhere, Jerry dove underneath everyone and secured the ball in those sure hands of his at our 18 yard line. Had Jerry not out-hustled the group of Cowboys who were after that ball, Dallas would have been in a position to turn the game around. Instead, Mike Bragg boomed us out of the hole and we put the clamps on the Dallas offense again.

Billy got us moving again late in the third quarter. Mixing tough runs by Larry with his own pinpoint passing, Billy moved us to the Dallas 45 by early in the fourth quarter. At this point, Mark Washington was at left cornerback for Dallas in place of Charley Waters who had been the victim of a broken arm while attempting to run back a punt. Billy again teamed with Charley Taylor to exploit Washington on a fly pattern for a 45-yard touchdown, giving us a 17-3 lead with about 14 minutes left to play.

The Cowboy offense was desperate, but so was our defense—we saw what was within our reach, and we weren't going off course at this late stage. In the huddle we kept encouraging one another: "Don't let us"; "Keep hitting"; "Hang in there." Then Calvin Hill was racked up going wide from his own 30 and he fumbled. Dancing Bear Ron McDole—the man whom people have been calling too fat, too slow, and too old for about four years now—pounced on the ball on the Dallas 38. Our offense didn't go anywhere, so Curt came in and kicked number two for the day for a 20-3 lead. The game was becoming a rout.

Curt went on to kick two more field goals, giving him four for the game, a playoff record. In the last six minutes of the game, we mopped up Staubach and the Cowboys. We were on top of the world, the first Redskin champions in 30 years. RFK Stadium was bedlam with spectators grabbing at us in the rain as we tried to make it to the locker room.

When we finally got inside, we quieted down long enough to hear this prayer of thanks by Tom Skinner: "Thank you for leading us this season. Thank you for a team of guys that hung together. Lord help us to be humble now that we are in a position of leadership." Then we went wild.

I was a little amused looking around at all the newsmen who were on hand. They were shaking our hands, congratulating us, and interviewing us. But I wondered how many of them had called us over-the-hill, or lucky, or figured we'd fade in our drive to the Super Bowl. In any case, it was good to see them, and people like Washington's Mayor Walter Washington and team president Edward Bennett Williams taking in our victory.

I dressed slowly, absorbing the feeling of victory. After considering various suggestions about how to celebrate our victory and New Year's Eve, Patti and I decided to join some other couples at a restaurant owned by retired Redskin Fran O'Brian. 1972 was good to us.

Happy New Year, Washington!

Roger-the-dodger looks for room, but can't find any.

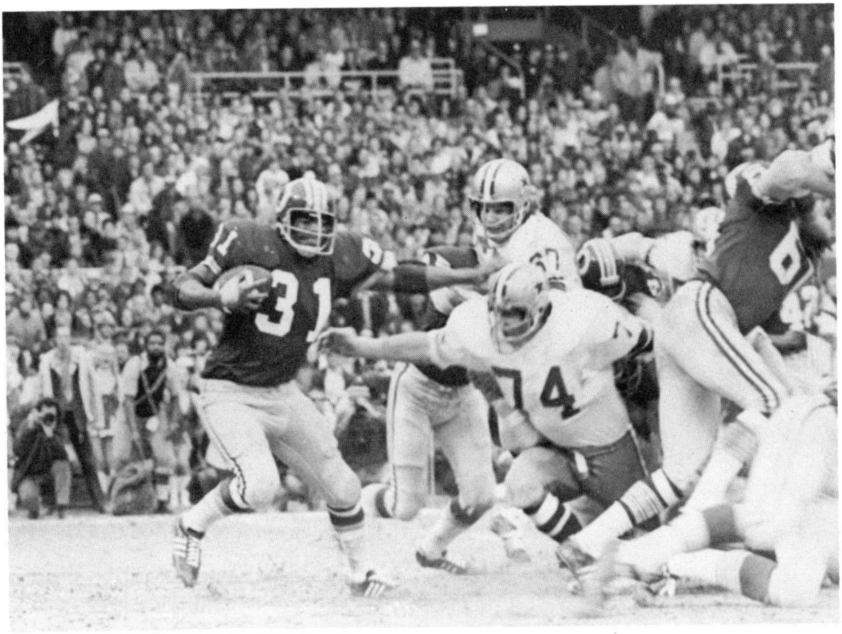

"Get back, Cowboys!" Charley Harraway looks for running room.

Ted Vactor deflects a Toni Fritsch field goal attempt in the championship game against Dallas.

Getting a crack at "crackbacker" Lance Alworth.

A jubilant George Allen, on the shoulders of Harold McLinton and Mack Alston, says, "On to the Super Bowl," after NFC Championship victory over Dallas.

The Super Bowl

Monday, Jan. 1

Somehow the hurts, aches, and pains of yesterday didn't bother me today. They were neutralized by a great feeling of accomplishment.

I watched some of the college games today, but I didn't pay very close attention. The only game that caught my eye for any length of time was USC vs. Ohio State. Southern Cal's Anthony Davis was dynamite. At times his running style and his appearance reminded me of Gayle Sayers. Of course, there will only be one Gayle Sayers. He did so many different things so well. But Davis is a good looking runner.

I dozed off to sleep while watching the games, and I was awakened by a news flash on television. The announcement said that Roberto Clemente, the great Pittsburgh Pirate outfielder, died in a plane crash near San Juan, Puerto Rico. Clemente was said to be on his way to help earthquake victims in Managua, Nicaragua. Roberto never seemed to get the publicity he deserved in his 18 years with the Pirates. His death is a great loss not only for the sports world, but for mankind in general. As I lay back down to continue resting, I had to wonder how things work. How could the Lord take the life of a man who was going to the aid of thousands of suffering people? The rest of the day was spent receiving intermittent phone calls from people wishing congratulations on yesterday's victory. I was also looking over statistics of the game, and they emphasized how thoroughly we dominated Dallas. We held Hill and Garrison to a combined total of 37 yards in 16 total carries. Staubach had 59 yards in five rushes, but 29 of those came on one run. We held Staubach to nine completions in 20 attempts. On our side of the stats, Billy had 194 yards, connecting on 14 of 18, and the touchdowns. Larry had 88 yards in 30 carries, and Charley Taylor caught seven of Billy's passes for 146 yards. These figures are hard to improve on. Dallas managed only eight first downs during the game, half our total, and in the second half the Cowboys never got further than their own 38 yard line. Incidentally, Alworth didn't throw one crackback block.

Tuesday, Jan. 2

The papers today said Coach Allen and his family visited President Nixon at the White House yesterday. Allen presented Nixon with a game ball from Sunday's game. I'd like to know who dominated the talking between two men as dedicated to their individual professions as those two are.

I told my two little girls before leaving for practice today that we will all soon be going to California to visit their grandmother. The Los Angeles grandmother is called Grandma, and the Cincinnati grandmother is Nanna. Robin can remember her last visit to Grandma's and how much she enjoyed it, but Tracy's a little too young to understand.

Everyone was loose at practice today. When Coach Allen came in someone said, "Coach, I hope you explained to the

President that, no disrespect intended, but we can't afford to use any of his plays against Miami." This was in reference to last year's playoff against San Francisco in which we ran an end-around drawn up by President Nixon that lost about 15 yards. Coach Allen assured us that no plays were discussed.

Coach Allen could hardly wait to get at the Dallas films. He said he feels Dallas would have been better off with Craig Morton instead of Staubach. He feels Morton is a little better play action quarterback and he also feels Morton had the rhythm going for the team. He concluded by saying, "It really wouldn't have mattered who the quarterback was. The way we played, no one could have beat us."

In the next breath, Coach Allen was talking about the Miami Dolphins. "They don't look flashy," he said. "They just beat people." In fact, they've beaten everyone so far this year and they sport a 16-0 record. The last time they lost was August 31 at RFK against us in an exhibition game. For most of the season, the veteran Earl Morrall led Miami. Morrall was called on after Bob Griese dislocated his ankle early in the season. But in their playoff game Sunday against the Steelers, it was Griese who pulled Miami to a 21-17 victory. We feel certain Dolphin head coach Don Shula will go with Griese in the Super Bowl.

At our team meeting Coach Allen announced that we would follow our normal practice schedule for the week, just as though our game was to be played on this Sunday. Then he surprised us all by saying he was giving everyone on the team a portable color television set for winning the NFC title. Not a bad little extra for us.

Coach Allen then outlined our program for next week. We'll be leaving for California on Sunday, Jan. 7. We'll stay at the Saddleback Inn in Santa Ana and practice at the Big A Stadium in Anaheim, about 10 minutes from my folks in Fullerton. I haven't been home for any length of time in about five years, and who could ask for a better homecoming than playing in the Super Bowl? I won't have much time to see friends and parents during our week of preparation, but after we win the Super Bowl, I'll have plenty of time. Meanwhile, I've already had requests for close to a hundred tickets. If I manage to get them, I can be sure that I'll be footing most of the cost. Honestly, I don't care about being paid back for this one; in fact, I'm happy just to be in the position to get tickets for my family and friends.

Coach Allen also talked about the distractions we would face in California, and there are plenty of them. Of course, Allen and several Redskins came to Washington courtesy of the Los Angeles Rams, so they have close ties on the West Coast. Although Coach Allen told us he feels we are mature and experienced enough to handle the distractions, I know he is concerned.

After we gleefully watched films of the Dallas game, Coach Allen got down to the business of preparing us for the Miami Dolphins. We reviewed their personnel and he pointed out how well Miami executes. Their runners are extremely talented. Fullback Larry Csonka is big, strong, and very tough, and Coach Allen said, "Csonka may not always look like he's doing much, but he always gets the yards." Mercury Morris is platooned with Jim Kiick at halfback. Morris is known for his speed and quickness, Kiick for his clutch running and ability to hold onto the ball.

Miami also has two fine quarterbacks. Earl Morrall is an experienced drop-back passer who had Super Bowl experience when he was with the Colts. Bob Griese is young with a good arm, the ability to run, and a lot of poise. He has Super Bowl experience from last year when Miami lost to Dallas.

Miami's most important receiver is Paul Warfield. He's the man who makes the big play. Coach Allen showed us a film on just Warfield alone. His smoothness and precision are truly remarkable.

Our workout was short but snappy. We practiced without any sign of letting up, although our game is nearly two weeks away.

Talby was teasing Double-O after practice asking him how many girl friends he had waiting for him in his home state of California. Double-O responded coolly, "Nothing you could handle, Talbert."

I went home and helped Patti and the kids pack. They are leaving for California tomorrow morning to stay with my mother. Before they left, we called Patti's parents in Cincinnati to invite them to the Super Bowl. Her father, a retired Cincinnati policeman known as Big Jimmy, said he can't get away from work, but her mother immediately said yes. She doesn't like to fly, so she's taking a train to L.A. to see the game. That's a real fan.

Wednesday, Jan. 3

I dropped Patti and the kids off at Dulles Airport this morning before practice. My daughters were incredibly excited. Robin told me, "Daddy, you be sure and hurry out to Granny's now." I assured her I'd see her soon. She tends to boss me a little. Like most Daddies, I listen.

Coach Allen said today he feels that Mercury Morris is the man who makes the Dolphin running game go because he can go inside and outside equally well. He's the man who keeps the defenses honest. We've also noticed that Miami doesn't throw to Warfield as often as people might think. Warfield's greatness comes from his ability in the clutch.

Today Coach Allen featured a film on Dolphin receiver Howard Twilley. Watching Twilley alone, we were impressed with his hands and moves. They more than make up for his slight lack of speed.

Hanburger was after Double-O on the practice field today. He stole his hat and said, "Hey, Double-O, do you think you'll be able to handle security in that Big-A Stadium? That's a lot of ground to cover."

Double-O grabbed his hat back and said, "Hanburger, you're the one who better worry about covering ground in L.A. Don't worry about me."

Practice was sharp again today. We're concentrating the way we should be.

My home is unusually quiet tonight. There are no little voices hounding me with questions and requests. Nor was anything cooking on the oven for me when I got in. It seems strange.

Thursday, Jan. 4

It's a good thing my mother taught me how to cook when I was younger. I was up extra early today fixing my own breakfast, but somehow, it didn't quite measure up to what I'm used to.

Coach Allen explained today that our defenses will be kept very basic for the Super Bowl game. We will concentrate on disguising our defenses so our coverages will always look different. Coach Allen has assigned one assistant coach the job of studying us on film and during practice to see if we're giving away any of our defenses. He checks out our stance, distance from receivers, the linebackers' positions along the line, and any other possible tendencies with which we might be revealing a defense.

We had a lot of hustle and concentration during practice despite light rain and cold temperatures. Towards the end of practice it began to rain harder and a few guys, without being told, went over and pulled the tarp over the field. We want to keep our field in good shape to practice on this week, so we took the initiative to cover it ourselves.

After working out, I munched a large piece of Duke Zeibert's Thursday victory cake and then went upstairs to watch more films. I watched our individual films on Warfield, Twilley, Briscoe, and tight end Marv Fleming, my main responsibility. Fleming is a blocker primarily, but he has a unique ability to determine when a defender is relaxing and then burn him. He's an old pro who played on the Lombardi coached Super Bowl teams. I made arrangements with defensive backfield coach Charley Winner to have a movie projector in my room in California so I can view the films on my own next week.

We picked up our television sets before leaving today. Guys whose wives are going to take a charter flight to California had to make arrangements today. Though the wives will fly as a group, they are not flying courtesy of the team.

Scalpers from Los Angeles were hanging around Redskins Park when I left. They know a lot of us need quite a few tickets, but I'm going to see if I can come up with my hundred some other way.

Friday, Jan 5

I studied films on my own early this morning at Redskins Park. I'm determined to know those Dolphins inside out. Film study is a habit I picked up as a high school and college quarterback. I find it very helpful.

Coach Allen said that our practices in California will be

completely closed. We'll have meetings in the early morning, followed by lunch, a press conference, and then our practice.

We reviewed our charts on the Dolphins and all of our important check points. Then Coach Allen showed a Dolphin vs. Cleveland Brown playoff game reel. Miami looked flat in that game for a while, but then they took charge. They came on to play with poise, like a champion is supposed to. They stopped Cleveland cold when they had to and played very tough football.

Practice was excellent again. Our two officials, Stringbean and Sully, have caught very few mistakes. It's unbelievable how sharp we are.

After practice I couldn't bear going home to the rigors of cooking dinner. Instead, I stopped and bought some fried chicken. I took it home, propped my feet up, and ate. Then I called California and checked in with my family. Patti said things are fine, and everyone's buzzing about Super Bowl VII.

Saturday, Jan. 6

This morning I couldn't face making my own breakfast, so I stopped on the way to Redskins Park. I'd go broke feeding myself as a bachelor.

Today's practice was set up just as though our game was tomorrow. Coach Allen believes in keeping a tight, careful schedule. He doesn't want us to follow any course which might vary from our regular way of doing things. So our workout was light, but spirited. We look sharper than ever.

Coach Allen got us all together in a team meeting today to remind us of our schedule for next week. He also cautioned us on taking care of ourselves and not forgetting our purpose. "There are already a lot of distractions in L.A.," he said, "but for us they'll be doubled by the fact that we're in the Super

Bowl. There will be a lot of extra attention focused on us." He then went on to say that there will be curfews in L.A., with fines for anyone breaking curfew.

One thing bothers me—it might be nice to have an extra week to rest, but honestly, I'd much rather play the game tomorrow. We're so used to football being a week-to-week thing, that our bodies have acquired a rhythm from which we hate to stray. I think I can now see why some past Super Bowl games were dull. Teams have a tendency to get stagnant instead of carrying the momentum they had in reaching the Super Bowl.

I played housekeeper tonight, trying to straighten up before I leave. One thing about this profession is that everyone knows when we're out of town. It wouldn't be hard for someone to stake out our house and we'd wind up coming home to a lot of empty rooms. So when we're going to be gone for any length of time, we get someone to stay in our house. This time, two college girls are handling the job.

California, here we come!

Sunday, Jan. 7

When I got to Redskins Park today, I found out that Coach Allen had cancelled our workout for today and that we'd only have meetings. So I went to our defensive meeting where Coach Allen emphasized our need to force mistakes in the Super Bowl. He's emphasized Miami's consistent play and reviewed our strategy.

In the locker room I checked to make sure I had my necessary items. I carefully packed all of my pads; I've had them for eight years and they're molded just right for my body. If I had to use another set, it just wouldn't be the same.

We were all taking our time getting our gear ready,

when we found out we'd be leaving earlier than expected. It seems a large crowd was beginning to gather around Dulles to see us off and Coach Allen wanted to avoid the confusion. So instead of leaving at 1:00 p.m. as was originally planned, we pulled a sneak play and left at 11:30 a.m. The crowd had grown to a pretty good size even at that hour and newspeople were all over the place. We could feel the electricity all the excitement was creating, and we were touched. Washington fans are so hungry for a winner, they are doing everything possible to cheer us on.

As we drove out of the Park, one enthusiastic fan was in the process of hanging a huge sign on a fence that had "Beat Miami" painted on it. When he saw our bus approaching, he panicked because he thought we wouldn't see the sign. So Coach Allen told the driver to stop the bus so that when the man finally finished, he turned to us and cheered, and we returned his cheer. Coach Allen really got a kick out of that incident. He laughed and said with enthusiasm, "These Washington people are just fantastic; there are no better fans than these in the world." We all agreed.

At Dulles, the entire airport was bustling with Super Bowl fever when we entered. The ticket clerks, stewardesses, and mechanics all wished us luck. Then, to top it all, as we entered the airplane we noticed that "Washington Redskins, NFC Champs" had been painted in big burgundy letters on the plane's nose. Inside, the plane was decorated with banners and balloons, and "Hail to the Redskins" was playing over the intercom system. The whole scene was a great thrill for me, but I kept reminding myself that it doesn't mean a thing until we go out and win that Super Bowl.

There was one thing wrong on the plane. It was a larger model than we usually fly, and we were unable to get our usual seats. We're all superstitious about where we sit, and take the same seats every time. But this time things were different, and a lot of guys were upset.

There was a small crowd waiting for us in L.A. A large group of media personnel was also there with cameras whirring. Everyone seems anxious to get in on the act and the game is still a week away. But it was good to see some familiar sights in L.A. as we drove to our hotel. Jerry was sitting in the back of the bus and he called out to me, "Hey, roomo, I sure hope you intend to take care of me out here. Get Roxy (my mother) to fix me a meal." His stomach always comes first.

When we pulled up to the hotel, there was a huge sign hanging out front saying, "Buenas Dias, Washington Redskins to Super Bowl VII." Things started to build inside me when I saw that, and I stepped off the bus into another crowd of people. I saw some familiar faces of personal friends. At the check-in desk there was a sign which read: "Welcome Home: John Wilbur, Bill Kilmer, Brig Owens, Jack Pardee, Myron Pottios, Diron Talbert..." and so forth, listing the names of all the players who were from the L.A. area. "This is really it," I said to myself, and I remembered what Sis said to me just before we landed in L.A. "Brig," he told me, "just think about how hard we've worked to get here; it's worth every bit of it." Amen, Big Sis, amen.

Since we were fatigued from the travel and excitement, Coach Allen called off our team dinner and meetings for the evening. I immediately telephoned Patti and she drove out to get me. My parents' house was filled with excited brothers, sisters, nephews, nieces, and friends. Tom Skinner came out with me and I think at some points he was awestruck at all the people. I had some of my Mom's good home cooking—ham, fried chicken, greens, etc. After a couple of hours I had Patti drive me back to the hotel. No wives are allowed to stay with players on this trip; they were considered a distraction. So I told Patti I'd call her when I got the chance.

Monday, Jan. 8

After a deep, sound sleep, I received a seven o'clock wake up call. We had a mandatory 8:00 a.m. breakfast, anyone missing it being subject to a $25.00 fine. Then we caught buses from the hotel to Anaheim Stadium for a 9:00 a.m. practice.

When we arrived at Big-A, we found out that the shoe distributor had sent us blue and white shoes. Our duffle bags were also blue and white and so were some of the tackling dummies. It didn't take much to figure out that whoever placed the order was expecting Dallas to be here instead of us— no faith in us right on down the line. Someone from our organization called another company, and they are going to supply us with red and white equipment more suited to our burgundy and gold colors.

Today was also press day and fan day at Big-A Stadium. After practice we had to stay on the field while newsmen and fans descended upon us. The place was a mob scene. One of my oldest buddies, Norman Perea, was the first person I saw on the field. Norm was one of these guys who always knew the neighborhood news before anyone else. He was like dust— always around. It was great to be able to rap with him for a few minutes.

I also saw Pete Laipis, a local Boys Club director who got me into organized sports. Without all his guidance, I doubt if I'd be where I am today. Pete told me how kids have changed now. "When you guys were coming through," he said, "I could punch or yell at you and know we'd still communicate. But now, if I yell at a kid, I've got a parent down my back." I notice that Pete complains, but he still is directly involved with the kids.

Before long we were literally overrun and we had to get

off the field while we could. Even though today was supposed to be a school day and the start of a work week, there must have been several thousand people who either played hooky or took the day off work.

Amid all the commotion, someone stole Coach Allen's hat, and one woman ran up and planted a big kiss on him. Actually things got a little dangerous because of the confusion, especially for guys nursing injuries or trying to avoid muscle pulls in the heat.

After we managed to arrive safe and sound in the dressing room, we were called out one by one for press interviews. No one was overlooked. When interviews were finished, we were on our own. I called Patti and went outside to wait for her, and to my surprise, thousands of fans were still out there waiting for us. Super Bowl excitement overtakes these people.

For the second night in a row I ate at my mother's with my family, but I tired out early. I returned to the hotel at 8:30 p.m., and Jerry was already in bed reading. He had visited with his mother, brother and sister, who were all down from San Francisco to see him, but he had gotten tired just as I had. We both felt the same way—the fatigue of talking to fans, newsmen, and family was as exhausting as any practice we'd been through.

Tuesday, Jan. 9

Jerry was kidding me this morning because my picture was on the front page of the sports section. "They sure can give a lot of pub to my rooms," he said.

"What do you expect for a home town flash?" I kidded back.

In a section of the paper called "Down Memory Lane" there was a story about John Huarte, a former high school star in Santa Ana and an All-American at Notre Dame. Jerry was reading parts of it to me, about how Huarte had completed 24 passes for 250 yards in a high school all-star game. They didn't mention that Huarte got beat that day—I was the quarterback who beat him. In that game I set an all-star game record throwing three touchdown passes and I also kicked the extra points. Through some shenanigans, Huarte was voted the game's MVP at halftime. Politics go on in sports from high school to pro ball, and I guess it will always be that way.

Jerry cut out a picture of Alvin Haymond signing autographs to put on the bulletin board at practice. Alvin is sitting there with a wide grin on his face in the picture. "That man sure can pose when he sees a camera, can't he?" Jerry said. Alvin *must* have known his picture was being taken; it's too perfect to be candid. Someone had put another picture on the board, of a guy lying in bed with a nude girl. The funny thing was that the guy looked *exactly* like one of our coaches. When the coach saw it, he said, "Now I know what kind of magazines you guys read around here." Someone commented to him, "Well, we don't have anything else to do; you guys keep us cooped up all the time."

On the early bus to Big-A Stadium, Coach Allen mentioned how pleased he was with the facilities. "They're so nice," he said, "I'll bet they thought the Dallas Cowboys were going to be here, but we fooled them." We fooled a lot of people.

Inside a little window in the stadium, Gabby noticed some little cocktail glasses with the California Angels insignia on them. "Those are the same size as the ones you got us last year," Jack said to Coach Allen. Coach Allen nodded. Then Jack went on with this hint, "It sure would be nice to have some larger ones this year." I think Coach Allen caught on; we need some larger glasses for our sets this year. It seems he's been giving out the same size glasses for years now.

Coach Allen expressed concern today at our generals meeting about everyone getting enough rest. He said he knows that some of the players won't realize what being out here means until it's all over.

At our team meeting Coach Allen gave us some guidelines about dealing with the super-sized press corps here. He told us to keep our patience answering their questions. He doesn't want their persistence to irritate us or make us forget about our goal here. Many of the guys have expressed the opinion that the interviews are a real pain in the ass. But everyone is trying hard to cooperate and being careful about not giving Miami any added incentive. I can really see why Coach Allen has said that if it was up to him, we wouldn't have come out here until Thursday or Friday.

At our defensive meeting today, Coach Allen showed a Dolphins film that was two years old. I don't know how he gets hold of these things, but he made some good points with it.

Jon Jaqua, one great specialty teams player, said today, "This is the most boring week I've ever spent. We work all day from nine to five and stay locked up all night, and we listen to the same questions from newsmen. I can't comprehend those sportswriters interviewing the same guys all week. It's a farce."

Len Hauss commented, "All that's really needed is the cotton candy and candy apples."

It's hard to plan things during the evenings because we never know when Coach Allen will call a meeting. But since my parents are only a few minutes away, I relaxed over there again tonight. When we returned to the hotel, I noticed special guards who have been assigned to watch our hotel. We immediately dubbed them "Double-O's Helpers."

Wednesday, Jan. 10

The word in the locker room today, along with ever-increasing bitching about the press, was that someone was caught jumping from a second story window—Jim Snowden, who has been on the injured reserve list since summer camp when he tore his knee cartilage. He has now picked up the nickname "Superman of the Super Bowl." It was an expensive jump for Snowman since he was hit with a $2000 fine. As someone put it, "That was an expensive piece of ass he almost got." Coach Lombardi used to say, "If she's that good, take me with you so I can see what she looks like for myself."

Coach Allen was extremely upset by the incident, even though he did cut the fine by $1000. In fact, he wanted to send Snowden back to Washington to keep him away from the rest of the team. Len Hauss told Coach Allen at our team meeting that the rest of the guys wanted Snowden to stay since he is part of our family. Coach Allen agreed, but I know it will be a long time before Snowman tries to take off again. I have to feel sorry for Jim and the rest of the guys who are here, but are ineligible for play; it's hard to face the same stringent rules the rest of us do. But Coach Allen did lay the cards on the table from the start, that everyone has to follow the same set of rules and pay the same price for breaking those rules.

When we got down to business at our meetings, it was mostly review. We set our strategy up last week and now we've just been going over our plans. Today we did check ourselves out on a film taken at one of our practices from last week, just to look for mistakes on our own.

After our daily dosage of press, we went out and had another good practice. Deacon Jones and Charlie Cowen, former players for Coach Allen when they were all with the

Rams, watched us practice for a while today. It's funny: I believe those two guys criticized Coach Allen's coaching techniques after he left the Rams for the Redskins. But today *they* were watching while George Allen's team practiced for the Super Bowl.

Jerry and I ate a huge Mexican dinner in our room tonight. Then I called Patti to tell her I was going out with an old buddy tonight, and she informed me that on January 20 the Fullerton Boys Club I spent so much time in as a kid is going to hold a Brig Owens Day. It made me feel good to know I'll be honored in such a way. When I told my roomo, he just shook his head and said, "M-a-a-a-n, you sure are big around these parts."

I went out with my friend tonight and sat around telling lies and drinking a couple of beers. When I returned, Jerry and I watched a couple of Dolphin films before knocking off for the night.

Thursday, Jan. 11

The stuff in the papers is unbelievable. Coach Allen and Coach Shula have been saying such complimentary things about each other's team, you'd think neither of them expected to score a point. Jerry said he hoped today would be the last day of the press meetings. I told him it could go on through Friday. "Impossible," he said. "They can't have any more questions to ask." Then he added, "They never talk to me anyway."

Coach Allen's irritation with the press is peaking. "Everyone wants to know the game plan," he said. "What makes them think I'd tell them?" He's also disgusted with the way newsmen keep bringing up his stint with the Rams. They won't just write that time off as history. It's like they're trying to get him to say something the L.A. fans will jump on.

Coach Allen said he has been playing around with the idea of using the five man line against Miami. "I want to look at it some more," he said, "but right now I think we might get burned in it." He pointed out that everyone knows Warfield, but there's a tendency to underestimate Howard Twilley. It's not like the Dolphins are a one-receiver team. I remember playing against the University of Houston when Twilley and quarterback Jerry Rhome were being touted as one of the country's top passing combinations. They were good, but we beat them too.

We focused our review on Miami's short yardage tendencies today. They are extremely tough going for short yardage, and they have the ability to turn short yardage plays into long gainers. Larry Csonka looks like he's only good for a yard or two, but he doesn't stop until he has four or five.

Our injury situation looks good. Terry Hermeling's knee, which he injured badly against Dallas, is coming around and he'll play Sunday. Everyone else seems healthy enough, and we all really appeared ready to go at practice. Our workout was very good.

When I got back to the hotel today, I found that some financial consultant had left a large stack of letters and brochures outside my hotel room door with a note instructing me to pass them out to the players. I didn't know the guy and he never even called me to ask if I'd do it for him. This is exactly the kind of stuff we try to avoid. These guys always have so much to offer us (according to them); they are all just dying to handle our money for us. This fella's material wound up in the trash.

I've heard rumors that certain major sporting goods companies are offering some Super Bowl players money to wear their products. I hope none of the guys will be foolish enough to go along with them. This is not the time to be breaking in a new pair of shoes or some other equipment. Why risk wearing something that might result in a mistake big enough to cost the game for a couple of hundred dollars? It's a lousy gimmick and a serious distraction. As Jerry put it, "Those companies are dangling a little hamburger in front of us when we've got a filet mignon waiting for us at the end of the line."

I relaxed at my mother's for a while and then returned to the hotel where Jerry was already waiting. The pressure of the game is starting to take its toll on everyone. Jerry said he's tired of being bugged by people, and I agree. We're getting restless for game time.

We each had a hot fudge sundae to settle ourselves. Actually, we each had one-and-a-half. Jon Jaqua was supposed to join us, so we ordered one for him. He was a little late showing up, so Jerry and I did the natural thing—we ate it. Jaqua arrived just as we finished his sundae, and he muttered something about us going to hell.

Friday Jan. 12

Jerry and I perused our morning newspapers and the pre-Super Bowl stories are still dominating the papers. Jerry said, "You'd think this game means more to some of the newsmen than it does to the players themselves."

I couldn't resist kidding Jerry, so I said, "Come on, rooms, you're just mad because you're not getting all the pub."

Jerry just laughed and said, "Well, I'll tell you, hometown-flash, everyone can have the publicity; I'll just take my Super Bowl ring and share and leave quietly."

Coach Allen had to miss our team meeting to go to a

press conference this morning. I know he was hot about that. Here it is two days before the biggest game of his career, and he couldn't be with his team. Len Hauss said, "I'll bet George is giving them hell."

When Coach Allen finally made it to practice, he was fuming. "Those newsmen don't have anything better to do than to ask the same questions time and again." Coach Allen told the newsmen at the start, "In all my years of coaching I've never missed a meeting with my team, and I'd like to get back to my ballclub." But naturally, they got their questions in.

Just to show how thorough George Allen is, he's hired someone to sit in the L.A. Coliseum this week from 12:30 p.m. to 3:30 p.m. This person's job is to watch the different angles of the sun during the time the game will be played and report them to Coach Allen. George Allen wants to be positive he knows everything possible about field conditions during the game.

After a good practice, Patti picked me up and we ate dinner with Tom Skinner and my brother Al who is in town for the game. I really enjoyed the evening and I actually did some real relaxing. I've felt cooped up all week. This week has been an extravaganza for everyone except the players; for us it has been all hard work and meetings.

Saturday, Jan. 13

We were given a day off from practice and the press today. We had our meetings in the morning, and then I went to my parents' place for a while. But before long, I got irritable and decided I'd better return to the hotel.

The team dinner was mandatory tonight. After we ate, Coach Allen reviewed tomorrow's itinerary. He pointed out that it's a 12:30 p.m. game, not a 1:00 or 3:30 game like we're used to. We don't want anyone walking in during the fourth quarter. Coach Allen then said, "After we beat Miami tomorrow, you guys can do all the carousing, visiting, and vacationing you want."

Jerry and I watched television for a little while and then we invited Tom Skinner over for our hot fudge sundae ritual. We also invited Jon Jaqua again, but he refused the opportunity to have his own. "I'll just eat a little from yours and Jerry's," he told me. Some guys get such pleasure in revenge.

Sunday, Jan. 14

For the third straight game day, I was up on my own and unable to eat much at the pre-game meal. I was on the first bus departing for the Coliseum, to get there early so I could take my time getting ready. I relaxed and concentrated on the game. Coach Allen called the generals in and reviewed our game plan.

We warmed up, went through our drills, and reviewed our plans once more before taking the field for the game we had spent most of our football lives trying to reach. And then, nothing worked for us.

For some reason, we were extremely flat from the very start. It's hard to figure because we had been so sharp in the playoffs and even in the practices. Sometimes in a game of this magnitude there's a tendency to try too hard. Our mistakes during practices had been almost negligible, yet during the game we made too many mistakes to win.

Miami's defensive line played an outstanding game. They took away our running attack by waiting for our offense to commit itself. That made it difficult to trap them and it weakened Larry's ability to cut back. Our offense couldn't move effectively, our specialty teams came apart in spots, and our defense had some bad moments. Yet, for as bad as we were, we held Miami to 14 points and I never doubted for a moment that we would find a way to beat them. Four more minutes, and I say we would have won that game.

There was one big key play early in the first quarter. We had noticed in our film study that the Miami center had a habit of lifting the ball off the ground and then placing it back down before snapping it. According to the rules, once the ball is lifted from the ground, it's in play. So we spent time practicing exactly what we would do if the situation came up in the game. We decided the middle linebacker, either Harold McLinton or Mo Pottios, would be in the best position to see the center. As soon as the ball was lifted, Harold or Mo would would go after it and the rest of the defense would react. Sure enough, in the first quarter Harold saw the ball go up so he blasted through and came up with it. We figured we had turned the ball over to our offense deep in Dolphin territory. But somehow, the official didn't see the ball leave the ground. Instead, he called an offsides penalty against us and Miami maintained possession. The situation never arose again.

Later in the first quarter, Jake Scott fumbled a punt, but we were unable to recover it. It turned out to be crucial, because Miami drove 65 yards in six plays for a touchdown. Griese set up the touchdown with a long pass to Warfield, and then he threw the touchdown pass, on a third and four situation, to Twilley. We were down 7-0.

The second quarter brought us more problems. We tried to get moving from our 30 but Larry and Charley Harraway found ground yardage hard to come by and we came up third and eight. Billy threw a pass that was picked off by Jake Scott. That got our blood boiling and we came out on defense and stopped Csonka twice and Kiick once. Miami was forced to punt.

We seemed to get on track late in the quarter, moving

from our 16 on the quick runs and passes that had worked so well during the regular season. On third and short yardage at the Dolphin 49, Billy popped a quick pass over the middle which the Dolphins veteran linebacker Nick Buonoconti intercepted and returned to our 28. The Dolphins converted that mistake into a touchdown with 18 seconds left in the half making it 14-0 at halftime.

I never doubted that we would overtake the Dolphins. Late in the third quarter, Larry Csonka broke loose and he got up a full head of steam going downfield. I had a good angle on Csonka in the open field and I was coming at his blind side, which also happened to be the side he was carrying the ball on. I knew he couldn't see me. I had only one thing on my mind—tackle the ball as hard as possible and knock it from his grasp. But someone else hit Csonka just as I made my move and he clamped down on the ball. The force of my hit did stop him, but only after a 50 yard gain. It was the longest run we had given up all year.

A few plays later from about five yards out, the Dolphins tried to score by throwing to their seldom-thrown-to tight end Marv Fleming. Fleming was my responsibility, and my instincts told me that Griese would be going to him. So when Fleming slid off the line, I let him slide inside of me, figuring I could beat him to the ball if it was thrown to him. That's exactly what happened. Griese threw for Fleming just as I anticipated. I dove for the ball and came up with the interception. At the time, I felt that maybe the play would turn things around. But it didn't.

The fourth quarter was wild. Our defense really dug in and we were holding the Dolphins. Billy got a good offensive drive going from our own 10. A pass to Roy Jefferson, a run by Larry, and a reverse to Jerry moved us to our 30. Then, on second and four, Larry broke off a 12-yard gain. Billy scrambled to midfield, while Charley Harraway picked up 12 yards on two consecutive carries. After a six-yard gain by Larry, it was third and inches on the Miami 32 and Larry picked up the first down on a four yard run. We finally seemed to look like the team that had played such flawless ball in the playoffs. The drive continued to the 10 on a run by Billy, a pass to Charley Taylor, and a run by Larry. Then, on second and seven, Billy's pass hit the crossbar of the goal post. His next pass was intercepted by Scott.

The Dolphins drove to our 35. Ted Vactor then forced a Miami mistake by blocking a Garo Yepremian field goal. Yepremian picked up the loose ball and batted it into Mike Bass' eager hands. Mike sped 50 yards into the end zone to make it 14-7 with just over 2:00 left. But our Super Bowl chances faded as the clock ticked away. Our mistakes had killed us.

Our locker room was solemn. Some men cursed, some threw things, some cried. I just sat in front of my locker and tried to get things together. George Allen said he was proud of us, and I believe he is.

Every man meets defeat from time to time. How he handles the setbacks is the true essence of the man. Victories are easy to accept. You laugh and cheer while others join you. But defeat—no one likes it. It tastes bad, and your entire being rejects it. Still, it has to be faced and considered a challenge. I know that's how this team will look at it. Throughout the off season this last game will stick in our minds. We'll return to camp next summer and we'll start our drive all over again. The specter of our Super Bowl loss will be just one more obstacle for us old fellows to overcome.

It was a great season.

We'll be back.

My attempt to steal the ball fails as Miami's Larry Csonka clamps down after spotting Jack Pardee.

My third quarter interception in the end zone brings hopes of turning the Super Bowl game around.